KOHELET

A MODERN COMMENTARY
ON ECCLESIASTES

by
LEONARD S. KRAVITZ
and
KERRY M. OLITZKY

UAHC PRESS
NEW YORK, NEW YORK

Library of Congress Cataloging-in-Publication Data

Kravitz, Leonard S.
    Kohelet : a modern commentary / by Leonard S. Kravitz and Kerry M. Olitzky.
        p. cm.
    Includes the text of Ecclesiastes in Hebrew and English.
    ISBN 0-8074-0800-X (pbk. : alk. paper)
    1. Bible. O.T. Ecclesiastes--Commentaries. I. Olitzky, Kerry M. II. Bible. O.T.
Ecclesiastes. Hebrew. 2003. III. Bible. O.T. Ecclesiastes. English. Kravitz-Olitzky. 2003.
IV. Title.

BS1475.53 .K73 2003
223'.8077--dc21   2002032227

Typesetting: El Ot Ltd., Tel Aviv
This book is printed on acid-free paper.
Copyright © 2003 by UAHC Press
Manufactured in the United States of America
10 9 8 7 6 5 4 3 2 1

Permissions

Every attempt has been made to obtain permission to reprint previously published material. The authors gratefully acknowledge the following for permission to reprint previously published material:

BRADLEY SHAVIT ARTSON: Excerpt from "Sunrise, Sunset" by Bradley Shavit Artson from *Learn Torah With . . . 3*, no. 5 (November 5, 1996). Reprinted by permission of Rabbi Bradley Shavit Artson.

LESTER BRONSTEIN: Excerpt "An eternity glows within our mundane selves . . ." from *the Bet Am Shalom Bulletin,* January 1994. Reprinted by permission of Rabbi Lester Bronstein.

CCAR: Expert from "Autonomy and Norms in Reform Judaism" by David Ellenson in *CCAR Journal: A Reform Jewish Quarterly,* spring 1999 and excerpt from "Personal Autonomy and the Sense of Mitzvah" by Peter Knobel from *Yearbook of the Central Conference of American Rabbis 96*. Reprinted by permission of the Central Conference of American Rabbis.

EDWARD FEINSTEIN: Excerpt from "The Tao of Judaism" by Edward Feinstein from Rosh HaShanah sermon, 1996. Reprinted by permission of Rabbi Edward Feinstein.

HARPERCOLLINS PUBLISHERS: Excerpts from *The Business Bible* by Rabbi Wayne Dosick. Copyright © 1993 by Rabbi Wayne Dosick. Reprinted by permission of HarperCollins Publishers Inc.

JEWISH LIGHTS PUBLISHING: Excerpt from *Being God's Partner: How to Find the Hidden Link Between Spirituality and Your Work* by Jeffrey K. Salkin. Reprinted by permission of Jewish Lights Publishing.

THE JEWISH PUBLICATION SOCIETY: Excerpts reprinted from *The Jewish Moral Virtues* by Eugene B. Borowitz and Frances Weinman Schwartz. Copyright date © 1999, by the Jewish Publication Society. Reprinted by permission of The Jewish Publication Society.

MA'YAN: Excerpt "Here is the truth: I am discontent..." by Sally Gottesman from "Changemaker Profile" fall 1998 www.mayan.org. Reprinted by permission of Ma'yan.

LEON A. MORRIS: Excerpt "There is an inescapable dialectic..." by Leon A. Morris from "Parashat Vayigash" eTorah, 2 January 2001. Reprinted by permission of Rabbi Leon A. Morris.

HAROLD M. SCHULWEIS: Excerpt from "Conversation with the Angel of Death" by Harold M. Schulweis from Rosh HaShanah sermon, 1991. Reprinted by permission of Rabbi Harold M. Schulweis.

SH'MA: Excerpt from "Leading by Example: Philanthropy and Transformation" by Lynn Schusterman from Sh'ma: A Journal of Jewish Responsibility 32/590, April 2002; excerpt from "Working with the Words of Torah" by Jane Rachel Littman" from Sh'ma: A Journal of Jewish Responsibility 31/579, April 2001; and excerpts from Sh'ma's publication Living Words: Best High Holiday Sermons of 5759 ed. Susan Berrin. For more information contact www.shma.com. Reprinted with permission of Sh'ma: A Journal of Jewish Responsibility..

HOWARD STEIERMANN: Excerpt "This is life's lesson..." from Rosh HaShanah sermon by Howard Steiermann. Reprinted by permission of Howard Steiermann.

Acknowledgments

There is something about *Kohelet*'s message that has intrigued both of us for many years. Our individual struggles to understand *Kohelet* began a long time ago, taking different forms and different shapes, and they continue to animate our friendship even as our work has taken us to different places over the last few years. It is the constant effort to make sense out of life, through the prism that *Kohelet* provides us, that brings us together as students, teachers, and colleagues to one another, to explore the timeless questions of *Kohelet*. It seems that we too are searching for answers to the same questions that *Kohelet* asks.

We thank our friends at the UAHC Press for inviting us to prepare another volume of classic text so that through its study our students in classrooms around North America may once again claim ownership of this wonderful book of biblical wisdom. We thank Ken Gesser, Stuart Benick, Rick Abrams, Debra Hirsch Corman, Liane Broido, Annie Vernon, and in particular, Rabbi Hara Person, who journeyed with us along the way and continues to encourage us to think deeply and widely so that all of our readers might benefit from the ancient wisdom of our Jewish teachers.

We also thank our friends, students, and colleagues at Hebrew Union College–Jewish Institute of Religion, New York, where our dialogue and friendship began nearly twenty years ago.

I want to also acknowledge my colleagues at the Jewish Outreach Institute (JOI) in New York. We have together built a community that encourages inclusivity and is welcoming to all. It is challenging work that bucks the complacency of many far more established institutions. It is an organization that understands the foundational text of the Jewish people to "welcome the stranger." In particular, I want to mention JOI's president, Terrence A. Elkes. His constant support of my ongoing efforts does not go unnoticed. I would be remiss if I did not also express my appreciation to my colleagues at JOI, especially Alex Unger, assistant executive director; Paul Golin, director of communications; and Ivana Bradanovic, office manager; as well as Hannah Greenstein, Denyse Gregoire, and Gail Quets. Working with a team of dedicated professionals, we have together created a model supportive community there. It is my prayer that our fledging efforts are duplicated elsewhere in the Jewish community.

Any words I write ring hollow without dedicating all that I do to my life's partner, Sheryl, and our sons Avi and Jesse. It is because of them that the sacred word resonates

deeply within my very being. There are no words that adequately express my love for them. Whatever I have become, and whatever I have yet to be, are a result of their unconditional love and unwavering support.
KMO

Since words of mine are inadequate to express what is in my heart, let me borrow some of Kohelet's. He wrote, *R'eih chayim im ishah asher ahavta,* which could be translated as "See life with the woman you love..." (9:9). This work and all else that I do is dedicated to my wife, Hanna, who has enabled me to fulfill Kohelet's advice and whose love has shown me life in all its aspects.
LSK

Rabbi Kerry (Shia) Olitzky
Rabbi Leonard S. Kravitz
Pesach 5761

Contents

Preface

In this volume, we propose to look at *Kohelet* (Ecclesiastes) as we might look at any classical text in Jewish tradition, trying to understand it and the world out of which it comes as best as we can, utilizing all of the classical commentaries as well as the scientific, more critical tools at our disposal. With each verse, we have to be aware that the text has a direct relationship with the world in which it was written. While *Kohelet*'s work is timeless, it was probably written about the third century B.C.E. So we begin our study of the text with a minimum of presuppositions, trying to read as much as possible out of it and as little as possible into it. Because we understand that this book has been part of the literature of the Jewish people and has had a place in its liturgy (we read it on Sukkot), we try to understand what Jewish scholars in the past read into the book and why they chose to do so. Since we now live in a postmodern world, the methods of investigation applied to other books help us to understand *Kohelet* in a more contemporary manner.

We have before us a book with an enigmatic title: *Kohelet,* a word that seems related to *k'hilah* (assembly, community). The word claims to be a proper name, the name of the son of David, king in Jerusalem—and the name of a king who himself ruled in Jerusalem. Such a claim presents the reader with a curious problem. We have no other information indicating that David had a son by that name or that a king by that name ruled in Jerusalem. While it is true that there have been political leaders in history who have been literary figures as well, the phenomenon is not widespread. It would be hard to imagine that a ruler with an unknown name, who ruled such a widely known place (Jerusalem) central to Jewish history, wrote a book using as a title the same unknown name. Jewish tradition (meaning the collective wisdom of the early Rabbis) seems to solve the problem by assuming that the book was composed by Solomon, son of David. This same Jewish tradition assumed that *Kohelet* was one of the three books written by Solomon. The others were Proverbs and Song of Songs.

For the reader not convinced by the traditional argument, the simplest hypothesis is that the book was written by someone who, for an unknown purpose, perhaps as a literary device, imagined himself as a "king" but who in fact was not "king in Jerusalem." Thus, the book's opening sometimes translated as "I, Kohelet, was king in Jerusalem over Israel" (1:1) can better be understood as, "I, Kohelet, have experienced as much as any person, including [King Solomon] the king of Israel in Jerusalem." The author is merely suggesting that no one has a better vantage point than he. And he would not be ready to judge had he not such a perspective on life. Perhaps it was written by a woman and such a device was absolutely necessary if anyone were to accept her words! Such a literary device, the taking on of an otherwise unknown name along with the claim that one is king, is already seen in part of a parallel literature. The Book of Proverbs is also ascribed to Solomon, specifically "Solomon, son of David, king of Israel" (Proverbs 1:1). However, in the last chapter of the book, a contradictory superscription is included, as well: "the words of King Lemuel." If the authorship of Proverbs can shed light on the authorship of *Kohelet,* perhaps we can assume that it is not autobiographical at all and is instead a work of fiction of sorts meant to edify its ideas, in part, by the pose of a king.

Nevertheless, to suggest that the book may be primarily fiction does not undermine its value for those of us who wish to gain from it guidance or spiritual insight. It is clear that the book seems to speak with many voices and in many styles. Perhaps it is indeed fitting that the book has as its Hebrew title the word *Kohelet,* suggestive of "community" or "assembly." As readers move through the book, they will discover that while there seem to be many voices in it, there are also shifts in styles and substance. For example, wisdom is praised as a goal, and then it is demeaned as futile. The narrator of the book—yet another voice—speaks of being raised to the pinnacles of power, only to be dashed to the depths of despair. One is bidden to enjoy good with the woman one loves and yet is told that the narrator finds women more bitter than death. The reader can easily understand why the Rabbis, noting the contradictions in the text, tried to suppress it (Babylonian Talmud, *Shabbat* 30b) and exclude it from the sacred literature of the Jewish people.

Theories abound to explain the disparate statements in the book. Some argue that the book, like Proverbs, is only a collection of different sayings by various teachers. Others maintain that there is a unity to the book, difficult as it may be at times to demonstrate it, that the different views may reflect the viewpoint of a principal author commenting on the views of others, or even such an author commenting on his own previously held views.

There is yet another factor in the discussion of the disparate views in this book. One might call it the pietistic factor. Although the Rabbis, as noted, discussed suppressing the book, they did not do so because, they said, "Its beginning was words of Torah and its end was words of Torah." While *Kohelet*'s "Torah" is clear at the end of the book in 12:13 (summarized as "revere God and keep the commandments"), it takes some manipulation to read the beginning as "Torah" in 1:3 ("What do you gain with all your work, with everything that you do *under* the sun?"). In order to bolster their claim, the Rabbis read "under" as "before."

Some in the modern world may attempt to harmonize elements in the book by reading into the text what may not be there. This is generally the case with the last verses of the book, often ascribed by scholars to be the work of a pious editor. However, we are referring to *Kohelet*'s use of the word "God" to indicate a religious attitude. To read that all things are in God's hands but that the same lot comes to the just and the injust (*Kohelet* 9:1–2) is to understand that for *Kohelet* the word "God" may suggest nothing more than "that is the way things are" and not suggest much of a religious attitude at all, as we have come to understand the term.

There were other reasons besides the possibility of different voices that moved some to recommend the suppression of *Kohelet*. In the midrash we read that "Rabbi Benjamin said, 'The Sages sought to suppress the Book of *Kohelet* because they found in it matters that inclined toward heresy" (*Kohelet Rabbati* 1:4). Although the midrash dealt with the supposed "matters that inclined toward heresy" in the same manner as the Talmud dealt with the issue of different voices (that is, by finding pietistic answers to the problem), the question remains as to whether the book really did "incline toward heresy." Moreover, we would want to ascertain whether the author of *Kohelet* was a heretic or a believer. While these terms are difficult to define, it is apparent that the religious approach of this book—of uncertain belief—differs markedly from the approach used by other books in the Bible. It is uncertain what the author believed about God, and we have no way of knowing whether the author believed what he wrote. The author speaks of God thirty-six times in the book. However, it is only in the last two verses of the book that God is spoken of in a manner consistent with traditional Jewish beliefs. Only there is the connection made between God and the commandments. As might be expected, many scholars see these last two verses as an add-on by the aforementioned pious editor/redactor.

It is hard to define the term "God" as it is used by *Kohelet*. Although we are told many things about God by *Kohelet,* we seem to miss the moral quality that we have come to expect in literary descriptions of the Deity. We are told that we should revere God, because all that God has done is perfect and can't be changed. Then we are led to understand that bad things, as well as good things, come from God. Wealth comes from God, but the ability to assign it correctly does not. The enjoyment of drinking comes from God, but God has troubled human beings by giving them an *inyan ra,* "a bad business" (1:13). God sets up everything properly. Yet, we are faced with wickedness in the place of justice. It seems doubtful that God justifies the innocent and condemns the guilty. Oppression occurs in this life, and one cannot be sure of the next life. We are told that all actions, whether of the righteous or of the wicked, are determined by God. Yet we are told that one should be careful of speech so as not to anger God. If you vow to pay something, then you should be sure to pay what you vowed. Even so, one should go carefully to the House of God.

These various statements about God reflect the nagging problem of different voices in the text. They also highlight the problem of the book's religiosity. There are verses that seem to be heterodox, and others—while not reflecting the general view of the Deity as articulated in the rest of the Bible—that are clearly not heterodox. God is presented by the author as ordering the universe as it is, in terms of natural processes, but is not presented as involved with a moral order. Readers are simply told to enjoy life and desire while young; yet, those same readers are told that they will be held accountable by God. How one is called to account is not clarified for the reader. The reader is to participate in the rites and rituals of Judaism—but not with too much enthusiasm. Perhaps this idea is the religious slant of the book: be religious; just don't be too enthusiastic about it. Such enthusiasm may blur your judgment and perspective on life and the world around you.

It would, therefore, seem appropriate to read *Kohelet* as carefully as possible, attempting to read everything we can *out* of it and to read nothing *into* it. We may note disparate sayings, contradictions, the change of views, and the change of style. We may even attempt to develop our own theories to account for the different voices, but we should indicate that these are only theories. There is no proof, as yet, to confirm any of them.

While one author of this translation (Leonard Kravitz) tries to read the book as objectively as possible and has no favorite theory to claim its authorship, his colleague (Kerry Olitzky) has indeed devised one of his own. He reads *Kohelet* through the eyes of an aged professor reflecting back on his life through the things that he has written down in a chapbook or taught during his life (and scribbled in lecture notes), what Olitzky likes to call "notebook jottings by the old professor." It is what the discipline of social gerontology might call "life review" or, in Jewish terms, *cheshbon hanefesh* (an accounting of the soul). The professor Kohelet continues to affirm in his old age some of what he observed in his youth. Other things he now rejects. The seeming contradictions are merely Kohelet's changes in opinions over the years of life and its experiences. It is the view of a more mature attitude toward life, one that has been seasoned by the years. It represents a lifetime of intellectual and emotional maturity without eclipsing the lessons learned in the early years—either from his own experience or the observation of the experience of others. We can easily envision an elder Kohelet musing over the pages of his diaries, repeating certain lines (even underlining or highlighting them) while rejecting others. His opinions have changed. We can even hear him speak of himself in the third person, something that we frequently heard our own teachers do when speaking of themselves, dogmatically, affectionately. The voice of the author, then, is Kohelet's own, and the second voice, the voice of the so-called editor, is also his own, writing from a perspective of some years later. The third voice, the voice of the second editor or redactor, is simply the one who readied this old professor's reflections for public consumption, perhaps a student or someone moved by his teachings. But this redactor also seems to be a God-fearing religionist who wants to bring closure to Kohelet's message so that it can be put into proper perspective before being presented to the masses. Perhaps this editor knew the real Kohelet and wanted to make sure that his or her teacher's words were framed in a way that could be appreciated. The editor/redactor accomplishes this with the final two verses in particular: "The last word, everything having been said and done: revere God and keep the commandments, for this applies to every person. God will bring judgment to every act, whether good or bad, even that which is hidden" (12:13–14). The dynamic perspective of the two translators of this volume is apparent in the commentary and explanation that follows each verse.

Regardless of who wrote the book, *Kohelet*'s wisdom must be discerned by us so that we can apply it to our daily lives. We try to understand it as if it had been written by one author. Readers may wonder what is to be gained by a book that begins "everything is useless" (or "all is futile," "all is vanity," or "everything is impermanent") and ends the same way. To be able to make such a statement is to know something that only humans can know. To say that "everything is futile" is to say that we have transcended the childish notion that we do good in order to get good. To say that "everything is impermanent" or vain is to know that however we view the world, whatever we think is the truth, there will come a better way—even if we will not be here to see it. All of us know that no matter how long we live, we will all die. Faced with death, one may say that all is futile, but this book instructs us to rejoice when we are young, and as we get older, it gives us an unblinking look at old age. Everything may be futile or impermanent or even vain, but to know that life is futile or impermanent is to realize that life is not! Moreover, it is only when we understand what we are and what we may become, particularly in relationship to the Divine, that we can gain real wisdom. And that is *Kohelet*'s essential message. When we learn what we are and our potential to make a difference in this world, even if "everything is impermanent," that's when it is possible to know that some things are indeed permanent.

Overview of Kohelet

Kohelet begins his message in chapter 1 by constantly repeating that nothing that happens is new. It has happened previously, and it will happen in the future. The sun rises and sets every day. Streams continue to flow into the sea, but the sea is never full. Even what we think is new is not really new. Ironically, *Kohelet* 1:2–11 is a repetition of the message that all life is repetitive. And even understanding this, as Kohelet does, is not helpful. Wisdom, according to Kohelet, only helps you to understand how worthless the pursuit of wisdom really is.

Understanding this, Kohelet attempts to provide the reader with a new approach to life. If life is merely a wisp of air, then why not enjoy the pleasures of the flesh! At first, this works for him. He increases his wealth and enjoys his lovers and his wine. But he concludes that this approach is no good either. All of us, rich or poor, end up in the same situation: dead and buried. At this point, Kohelet begins to suggest to the reader God's role in this fruitless plan. He notes that although there is nothing inherently good about enjoying wine and wealth, it all comes from God. Thus, there must be some logic to this life.

And Kohelet begins to understand the fatalism he has observed in life. He ascertains that there is a time for everything, and it is in accordance with the plan of the Deity. Yet, Kohelet struggles with the notion that evil exists alongside righteousness. He concludes that this situation is the fault of humans, not God. Humans may not be able to dominate the beast (wickedness) that exists inside the soul, but it does not matter. Both are destined for the same fate: death. And no one knows what lies beyond death.

Kohelet continues, analyzing the value of human contribution, noting that all labor is in vain, the result of human envy of one's neighbor. This time, he adds another element to the human lot: companionship. For Kohelet, an individual requires a lifelong companion in order to survive.

Next, Kohelet analyzes God in the role of judge. This is a common biblical motif. He concludes that each individual's life is determined by many factors, but all of these factors are controlled by God. They always have been and always will be.

The author shifts his message into a different idiom in chapter 7. At this point, he provides the reader with a list of practical maxims. Kohelet concludes that his wisdom, however profound it may be and helpful for other people, is superficial. In order to truly understand the mysteries of the world, one must understand the logic of Deity, and this is beyond any individual's comprehension.

The theme of wisdom abounds throughout the next two chapters. Kohelet attempts to provide the reader with guidance culled from the insights he has drawn in his life. This culminates toward the end of chapter 11, where Kohelet cries out, "Be happy, young person, while you are young.... Because the prime of youth evaporates" (11:9–10). Kohelet has accepted mortality. Knowing what it means, he advises us that one should always enjoy life, because the "days of darkness" (11:8) or sorrow eventually come for everyone. Old age for Kohelet becomes a well-conceived metaphor. Old age as metaphor can come to an individual at any time, at any age. It is then that there will be no pleasure for the individual.

Kohelet effectively uses many metaphors throughout the volume, but the metaphor of old age is especially striking. He describes the old person in many ways, but one message emerges in every image: the body is in a state of rapid decay. For Kohelet, the term "old age" is pejorative because it refers to the negative experience of bodily decline, but it does not refer to a specific chronological age. For him, "old" refers to a specific individual approach to life. For Kohelet, there is in old age a waning strength of specific organs; the image of a blotting out of life as an advancing storm; the approach of death as the advance of night; and the decay of vitality as the ruin of a wealthy estate. Kohelet knows all of these, because, at the time he is writing, he too is old. He has realized that *hakol havel,* "everything is useless" (12:8). But the editor of *Kohelet* is unsatisfied leaving us with such a thought. Instead, he wants us to believe that we are all accountable to God for our actions no matter how futile they seem to be—even if the description of God earlier in the book may suggest a different image entirely.

Introduction to This Volume

Kohelet is a book of *chochmah,* "practical wisdom." It offers the reader guidance for daily living. The author placed a high priority on the Greek notion of rhetoric, a notable influence in his work. As in Egyptian tradition, the author placed his wisdom in the mouth of a king (Solomon) to give it authority. Whoever the author really was, the Book of *Kohelet* is the work of an intuitive, insightful individual who has a passion for life, having lived a long and rich life. He probably compiled the book in his old age and reports on observations in his own voice, as well as the voice of a narrator, that is, the old man Kohelet.

Kohelet was motivated, as we are, to write by his observations in life, the same life that each individual experiences. The human condition has changed little since his time. Kohelet's twelve chapters are randomly divided into a loose collection of maxims, sayings, and observations. But they are generally compiled in individual units that cannot be separated from one another. For the editor, faith in God transcends the earlier message of Kohelet that life is meaningless. There is skepticism and tired resignation, but there is also an abiding faith. And there is a desperate struggle to understand his own observations. Kohelet is old, perhaps approaching death. He is trying to make sense of his own life. In doing so, he provides us with a message that we seek to understand in this volume, aided by the classic commentators of Jewish history.

As we have done in our previous translations and commentaries of classical texts, we have chosen from among the classical commentators available for study. We have made primary use of the works of Rashi, Abraham ibn Ezra, and Gersonides. They represent three different perspectives on this text and on others, as well as on Jewish life. We often add the perspective of Maimonides, as the pivotal thinker in the history of Jewish thought. We also include insights that emerge from the interpretative Aramaic translation of the Bible known as the *Targum.* On occasion, we take guidance from the *Biblia Hebraica,* a familiar critical edition of the Bible edited by Kittel. Finally, we take some direction from the critical scholarly work of Koehler and Baumgartner and regularly consult their references. As a result of this approach, we intend to provide a new translation and commentary in a modern idiom, familiar to our readers. This approach will make the text and its wisdom readily available to all who would turn its pages. Along the way, we will add our own comments, those that surface from the depth of our own experience, as well as those that are provoked by our reading of the text. These will further help us to understand the profound spiritual meaning of the text so that it can shed divine light on our daily lives.

A Note about the Gleanings

While we have endeavored to choose those selections that are gender sensitive, some of the entries in the gleanings sections came from an era prior to the awakening of gender sensitivity. They are included, with apology, because of their important message.

CHAPTER ONE

א:א דִּבְרֵי קֹהֶלֶת בֶּן־דָּוִד מֶלֶךְ בִּירוּשָׁלָ͏ִם:

1:1 THESE ARE THE WORDS OF KOHELET, SON OF DAVID,
KING IN JERUSALEM.

The writer apparently attributes his work to King Solomon. Perhaps this is merely a statement that suggests a vantage point to the reader: I am Kohelet, the one who assembled these words. I take the perspective of a son of David, who was king in Jerusalem. Identifying Kohelet as Solomon, the *Targum* considers the book to be the embodiment of his words of prophecy. Rashi follows the *Targum* and claims that the name Kohelet is derived from the root *kahal* (to gather), a suggestion that Solomon *gathered* all kinds of wisdom.

א:ב הֲבֵל הֲבָלִים אָמַר קֹהֶלֶת הֲבֵל הֲבָלִים הַכֹּל הָבֶל:

1:2 "IT IS ALL USELESS, KOHELET SAID, IT IS ALL USELESS.
EVERYTHING IS USELESS."

Alternatively, "Everything is impermanent, said Kohelet, it does not last. Nothing endures." This statement, "*haveil havalim, hakol havel*," and its primary root word *(hevel)* have been translated in numerous ways: vanity, nothingness, vapors. However it is to be translated, *hevel* is somewhat oxymoronic. It is somehow something that is nothing. Its sense is somewhat of an ennui that is difficult to translate into English. While most translations use the phrase "vanity of vanities," the English connotations surrounding the word "vapor" distract the reader from its denotation of "empty." The *Targum* explains *haveil havalim* as Solomon despairing over future events: the kingdom will be divided, the Temple will be destroyed, the Jewish people will be dispersed; all that for which Solomon and his father have labored will have been in vain.

א:ג מַה־יִּתְרוֹן לָאָדָם בְּכָל־עֲמָלוֹ שֶׁיַּעֲמֹל תַּחַת הַשָּׁמֶשׁ:

1:3 WHAT DO YOU GAIN WITH ALL YOUR WORK, WITH
EVERYTHING THAT YOU DO UNDER THE SUN?

This translation avoids the common gender-specific translation: "What gain does a man have?" The basic meaning of *yitron* (gain, benefit) is "what is left over." It is a word that seems to reflect what Marx had in mind when he spoke of "surplus value." What has the individual got left after a lifetime of accumulating? You can keep it up,

1

but you can't take it with you when you die. *Amal* (gains) refers to both the labor and the accomplishments that result from the labor. The *Targum* seeks to temper the despair of the verse and move it toward a more "religious" point of view by adding to it: "What does one gain after death from all one's labor in this world beneath the sun?" The *Targum* continues, "By engaging in Torah study, one will receive a reward in the presence of the Master of all in the world-to-come." Following the *Targum*, Rashi relates "under the sun" to the Torah itself.

א:ד דּוֹר הֹלֵךְ וְדוֹר בָּא וְהָאָרֶץ לְעוֹלָם עֹמָדֶת׃

1:4 ONE GENERATION GOES AND ANOTHER GENERATION
COMES. BUT THE EARTH ALWAYS REMAINS THE SAME.

People are born; people die. It is as if you were never born. The only thing that lasts is the earth itself. Ibn Ezra sees the "earth" in this verse, the "sun" in the next verse, the "wind" in verse 1:6, and the "rivers" in verse 1:7 as allusions to the four basic elements, in other words, earth, fire, air, and water. It was believed that all things were derived from these elements and would return to them. Rashi sees a modicum of consolation in the verse: what the wicked may acquire in one generation will be lost to their descendants in the next generation.

א:ה וְזָרַח הַשֶּׁמֶשׁ וּבָא הַשָּׁמֶשׁ וְאֶל־מְקוֹמוֹ שׁוֹאֵף זוֹרֵחַ הוּא שָׁם׃

1:5 THE SUN RISES AND THE SUN SETS, AND GLIDES BACK
TO WHERE IT RISES.

The image is simple: the sun is presented as if on a treadmill. The sun sets in the evening and runs around the earth to get to the place where it will rise the next morning. The movement of the sun, the blowing of the wind, and the flowing of the rivers are all constant and meaningless motion. They seem purposeful, but they are not going anywhere. Reflective of the tedium of nature, they constantly repeat the same things, every day. Everything moves in circles, and nothing really changes. Our lives are the same way. Things move and nothing has really changed.

א:ו הוֹלֵךְ אֶל־דָּרוֹם וְסוֹבֵב אֶל־צָפוֹן סוֹבֵב סֹבֵב הוֹלֵךְ הָרוּחַ
וְעַל־סְבִיבֹתָיו שָׁב הָרוּחַ׃

1:6 GOING TO THE SOUTH, THEN TURNING NORTHWARD,
THE WIND GOES AROUND AND AROUND, AND ON ITS
ROUNDS, THE WIND COMES BACK.

Ibn Ezra notes that seafarers are able to use the motions of the wind to carry them on their journeys. Kohelet notes that while the wind seems to make progress, after all its exertion, it ends up where it started.

אː‎ז כָּל־הַנְּחָלִים הֹלְכִים אֶל־הַיָּם וְהַיָּם אֵינֶנּוּ מָלֵא אֶל־מְקוֹם שֶׁהַנְּחָלִים הֹלְכִים שָׁם הֵם שָׁבִים לָלָכֶת:

1:7 ALL RIVERS FLOW INTO THE SEA. YET THE SEA IS NEVER FULL. TO THE PLACE WHERE THEY FLOW, THE RIVERS FLOW BACK AGAIN.

The sea is similar. It appears one-directional. But why does it never fill up? Somehow, the water returns to the sky as rain and fills the oceans. The author realizes that water is a closed system of some sort. Both Rashi and the *Targum* suggest that the waters flow back through an underground tunnel system. According to Ibn Ezra, the endless cycle of rivers running into the sea, which is never filled, is explained by evaporation. Water from the sea is drawn up by evaporation into the clouds. The clouds bring rain. The rain is carried into the rivers, and the rivers run into the sea. Thus, rain and rivers and the sea are part of an unchanging cycle.

אː‎ח כָּל־הַדְּבָרִים יְגֵעִים לֹא־יוּכַל אִישׁ לְדַבֵּר לֹא־תִשְׂבַּע עַיִן לִרְאוֹת וְלֹא־תִמָּלֵא אֹזֶן מִשְּׁמֹעַ:

1:8 EVERYTHING IS EXHAUSTING. YOU CAN'T SPEAK. THE EYE CAN'T SEE ENOUGH. THE EAR CAN'T HEAR ENOUGH.

Nevertheless, we are not ready to call it quits. Our eyes never get enough, nor do our ears. We try to understand. We are never satiated, but we go around in circles. The future merely repeats the past. There is eternal return. There is no novelty in the system, but somehow we still want to go on living.

אː‎ט מַה־שֶּׁהָיָה הוּא שֶׁיִּהְיֶה וּמַה־שֶּׁנַּעֲשָׂה הוּא שֶׁיֵּעָשֶׂה וְאֵין כָּל־חָדָשׁ תַּחַת הַשָּׁמֶשׁ:

1:9 WHAT WAS IS WHAT WILL BE. WHAT HAS BEEN DONE IS WHAT WILL BE DONE. THERE IS NOTHING NEW UNDER THE SUN.

This statement reflects a rather comfortable life. The one who is working desperately just to survive does not regard the changelessness of life so placidly. Although the author thinks that nothing really changes, he seems eager to want to be around to see how things turn out. Perhaps something new may yet happen after all.

3

א:י יֵשׁ דָּבָר שֶׁיֹּאמַר רְאֵה־זֶה חָדָשׁ הוּא כְּבָר הָיָה לְעֹלָמִים אֲשֶׁר הָיָה מִלְּפָנֵנוּ:

1:10 THERE MIGHT BE SOMETHING THAT ONE MIGHT SAY,
"LOOK! HERE IS SOMETHING NEW!" BUT IT ALREADY
HAPPENED A LONG TIME AGO, BEFORE OUR TIME.

The Rabbis used this statement to justify the Oral Law: "Whatever a scholar may deduce, this too was spoken to Moses at Sinai" (*Vayikra Rabbah* 22:1; *Kohelet Rabbah* 1:29 et passim).

א:יא אֵין זִכְרוֹן לָרִאשֹׁנִים וְגַם לָאַחֲרֹנִים שֶׁיִּהְיוּ לֹא־יִהְיֶה לָהֶם זִכָּרוֹן עִם שֶׁיִּהְיוּ לָאַחֲרֹנָה:

1:11 NO ONE REMEMBERS THOSE WHO WENT BEFORE, AND
NO ONE WILL REMEMBER THOSE WHO COME AFTER,
EVEN BY THOSE WHO COME AFTER THEM.

Generations come and go, only to be lost in oblivion. There is no *zichron* (trace) of any of them. And there will be no trace of the later ones after they have passed. The *Targum* is even more melancholy: not even the very last generation—prior to the onset of the messianic era—will leave a permanent mark on the world. In other words, neither the individual nor the species will leave a mark on the "sands of time."

א:יב אֲנִי קֹהֶלֶת הָיִיתִי מֶלֶךְ עַל־יִשְׂרָאֵל בִּירוּשָׁלָם:

1:12 I, KOHELET, WAS KING OVER ISRAEL IN JERUSALEM.

The author takes on the identity of the most influential king in the history of the Jewish people. He suggests that no one has a better vantage point. He has experienced as much as any person (including King Solomon). He would not be ready to draw any conclusions about life had he not had that perspective. Both Rashi and the *Targum* explain the force of the phrase "was king." While both take Kohelet as Solomon, Rashi understands the verse to mean that Solomon once reigned as king over Israel and much of the world, but when he wrote this book, he was no longer king. The *Targum* goes on to explain why he was no longer king: Solomon had sinned. Puffed up with pride, Solomon had amassed too much money, gathered too many horses, and married too many pagan women. As a punishment, God sent Ashm'dai, king of the demons, to drive Solomon from his throne. Repentant and in tears, Solomon went from place to place within his former kingdom, saying, "I am Kohelet, who used to be called Solomon, who was king over Israel in Jerusalem." Ibn Ezra accepts the notion that this book was written by someone looking back over his life. He adds an analysis of those areas that have the right climates in which wisdom can develop. According to Ibn Ezra, it is only possible in more temperate zones, for a medieval belief about anatomy held that if you got too cold or too hot, you would cook off the humors, basic elements in the body, and hence not be able to function properly.

וְנָתַתִּי אֶת־לִבִּי לִדְרוֹשׁ וְלָתוּר בַּחָכְמָה עַל כָּל־אֲשֶׁר נַעֲשָׂה תַּחַת א:יג הַשָּׁמָיִם הוּא עִנְיַן רָע נָתַן אֱלֹהִים לִבְנֵי הָאָדָם לַעֲנוֹת בּוֹ:

1:13 I SET MY MIND TO INVESTIGATE AND WISELY EXPLORE EVERYTHING THAT OCCURS BENEATH THE HEAVENS. IT IS A BAD BUSINESS THAT GOD HAS GIVEN HUMANS WITH WHICH TO CONCERN THEMSELVES.

The heart *(lev)*, which we translate as "mind," was considered to be the point of wisdom. Perhaps Kohelet meant "heart" the way we mean it today when we say, "His heart was in it." Ibn Ezra connects this verse with the next in order to explain it.

רָאִיתִי אֶת־כָּל־הַמַּעֲשִׂים שֶׁנַּעֲשׂוּ תַּחַת הַשָּׁמֶשׁ וְהִנֵּה הַכֹּל הֶבֶל א:יד וּרְעוּת רוּחַ:

1:14 I TOOK NOTE OF EVERYTHING THAT HAPPENED UNDER THE SUN. I FOUND EVERYTHING TO BE USELESS AND AN EMPTY PURSUIT.

The *Targum* translates *r'ut ruach* as *tevirat,* a rather vulgar expression for what we translate as "empty pursuit." This is usually translated as "striving after wind" or "breaking of the spirit" and is probably just a pallid euphemism for something more reflective of bodily function. Kohelet's search for understanding is frustrating. It is a "will-o-the-wisp," as is everything else. Everything ends up in frustration. The attempt to understand is an affliction of the human species that never abates. Then Kohelet gives us a survey of his experiences. Whatever he saw and did was futile, chasing after things that were wind, empty.

מְעֻוָּת לֹא־יוּכַל לִתְקֹן וְחֶסְרוֹן לֹא־יוּכַל לְהִמָּנוֹת: א:טו

1:15 A CROOKED THING CANNOT BE MADE STRAIGHT. WHAT IS MISSING CANNOT BE COUNTED.

Some things cannot be fixed. One may want to read this verse as a continuation of the image suggested by "bad business." If so, the writer is suggesting a reality of commerce: If a customer expects something to be straight and it is crooked or twisted, he or she will not buy it. A customer who expects to buy something and discovers a flaw may not buy the item at all rather than calculate the value and request a discount. If such defects affect business, then they also affect life. Crooked is crooked, and a deficiency can never be made up. One cannot turn a minus into a plus. One cannot make a straight line out of a curve. There is no possibility for change. Ibn Ezra relates this verse with the phrase "beneath the heavens" in verse 1:13. He sees an astrological connotation: one who is born in a deficient array of the constellations will be unable to perfect his or her soul.

א:טז דִּבַּרְתִּי אֲנִי עִם־לִבִּי לֵאמֹר אֲנִי הִנֵּה הִגְדַּלְתִּי וְהוֹסַפְתִּי חָכְמָה עַל כָּל־אֲשֶׁר־הָיָה לְפָנַי עַל־יְרוּשָׁלִָם וְלִבִּי רָאָה הַרְבֵּה חָכְמָה וָדָעַת:

1:16 I SAID TO MYSELF, "I HAVE GROWN RICHER AND WISER THAN ANYONE WHO HAS RULED OVER JERUSALEM BEFORE ME, AND MY MIND HAS ABSORBED GREAT WISDOM AND KNOWLEDGE."

Where does this understanding lead the individual? Nowhere. It is as if Kohelet is saying, "I have reached great eminence and gathered more knowledge than anyone before me, and I have gained nothing." Rashi puts these words in Solomon's mouth: "After I achieved so much, how did I come down so low?"

א:יז וָאֶתְּנָה לִבִּי לָדַעַת חָכְמָה וְדַעַת הוֹלֵלוֹת וְשִׂכְלוּת יָדַעְתִּי שֶׁגַּם־זֶה הוּא רַעְיוֹן רוּחַ:

1:17 SO I SET MY MIND TO ASCERTAIN WISDOM AND KNOWLEDGE, AS WELL AS MADNESS AND FOLLY. AND I LEARNED THAT THIS TOO IS AN EMPTY PURSUIT.

Perhaps Kohelet's goal is to understand a pursuit of nothing or nothingness. In his personal journey, he realizes that the more you learn, the more painful it is to know that you don't really know anything. "Wisdom and knowledge" is parallel to "madness and folly." Rashi notes that wisdom may become madness if you decide to depend on your own wisdom and not avoid what is prohibited.

א:יח כִּי בְּרֹב חָכְמָה רָב־כָּעַס וְיוֹסִיף דַּעַת יוֹסִיף מַכְאוֹב:

1:18 THE MORE WISDOM, THE MORE GRIEF. THE MORE KNOWLEDGE, THE MORE PAIN.

Ibn Ezra notes that our understanding of reality brings grief as we realize our own mortality and the mortality of those we love.

Oral Law

The term "Oral Law" refers to the interpretation and analysis of the Written Law (Torah) handed down orally from generation to generation. It is a general reference to the Talmud. Jewish tradition teaches that the Oral Law was given at Sinai at the same time the Written Law was given to Moses. However, critical scholars suggest that the Oral Law is the accumulated classroom discussions of the rabbinic academies, written down as the Mishnah in the year 200 C.E. The Gemara, in which the Rabbis discuss the Mishnah, was written down to form the Talmud (in two versions: one in Babylonia, completed ca. 500 C.E., and one in the Land of Israel, ca. 400 C.E., sometimes referred to as the Palestinian or Jerusalem Talmud).

Wisdom

Wisdom has meant a variety of things during the history of Jewish thought. In the Bible, wisdom refers to a specific grouping of literature that suggests a pragmatic and prudential view of ethics. These books, *Kohelet,* Proverbs, and Job, reflect a view generally paralleled by other Near Eastern Literature. During the rabbinic period, Rabbis used the term "wisdom" to refer to Torah, particularly the Oral Torah (or Oral Law), as the rabbinic method of understanding the Written Torah. Whether or not this Oral Torah was given at Sinai, passed down orally, or written down, it was only a taste of the sublime divine wisdom. Divine wisdom was understood by medieval philosophers as the essence of the Deity. Some philosophers understood divine wisdom as the sum total of all possible knowledge. They believed that individual thinkers—through training and diligence—could achieve activation of their own intellects and apprehend some bits of divine knowledge and thereby come into contact with the Divine intellect.

Regardless of whether it was in the biblical, rabbinic, or medieval mind-set, wisdom was the goal of learning. The writer of Proverbs put it this way: "Wisdom begins with getting more wisdom" (Proverbs 4:7). Throughout their history, Jewish people have sought wisdom. They believe that they could "get wisdom" by studying Torah; by studying Torah, they might understand the world and the Ultimate Value behind it. And that is the basic motivation behind seeking wisdom.

Adapted from Leonard Kravitz and Kerry Olitzky, *Shemonah Perakim: A Treatise on the Soul*
(New York: UAHC Press, 1999), 61

GLEANINGS

People and Their Work

Because we spend so much time working, we should consider what Jewish tradition tells us about work. We read in Genesis that in the Garden of Eden, Adam and Eve did not have to work. All that was needed to sustain life was available to them without toil. After Adam and Eve disobeyed God by eating the fruit from the Tree of Knowledge, God declared: "Cursed be the ground because of you; by toil shall you eat of it all the days of your life: Thorns and thistles shall it sprout for you.... By the sweat of your brow shall you get bread to eat" (Genesis 3:17–19).

Adam and Eve must have felt the harshness of God's punishment. Having never worked, now they had to struggle to survive. However, the question for us is: Should we see God's punishment as a curse today? The sages viewed work as part of the divine plan from the beginning. Rabbi Simeon ben Eleazar said, "Even Adam tasted nothing before he worked. The Scriptures say, 'And God put him into the Garden of Eden to till it and to tend it.' Only after that did God tell him, 'Of every tree in the Garden of Eden you may freely eat'" (*Avot de-Rabbi Natan*, chap. 11). According to the rabbis, work did not diminish the pleasure of living but enhanced it.

Allan C. Tuffs, *And You Shall Teach Them to Your Sons: Biblical Tales for Fathers and Sons* (New York: UAHC Press, 1997), 85

The Natural World Order

In its continuous unfolding, the natural world is the context within which life proceeds. As death separates us from God, it also emphasizes those aspects of our humanity which separate us from nature. Nature embodies a process of death and rebirth that gives it the appearance of being actually deathless: it symbolizes the immortal. The experience of death ends our experience of ourselves, of our consciousness. Because of this, we alone are fully mortal.

As a symbol of the immortal in this world, nature, like God, can provide moments-of-life without death for people to reflect upon. The depth of our response to the beauty of a natural scene or the peace experienced by our sense of nature's order helps to anchor us in a larger frame of reference for our lives. Just as we can deny the presence of God by expanding the moments-of-death in our lives, so, too, we can deny the life-affirming potential of nature by expanding the moments-of-death in relation to it.

Ira F. Stone, *Seeking the Path to Life: Theological Meditations on God and the Nature of People, Love, Life, and Death* (Woodstock, Vt.: Jewish Lights Publishing, 1992), 53

Wisdom

Sechel, literally, "wisdom." *Sechel* means more than book learning, more than acquired knowledge. *Sechel* means deep understanding and insight; the ability to perceive and discern. *Sechel* means having common sense and "street smarts"—having the capacity to meet any challenge and to prevail through wisdom and wile. Every day we need to use our own *sechel* and to surround ourselves with people who have *sechel*.

Wayne Dosick, *Soul Judaism: Dancing with God into a New Era* (Woodstock, Vt.: Jewish Lights Publishing, 1997), 94

Afterlife

What happens to the divine Image after death? It takes on other forms. The Image that in life is taught by word and deed is transformed into afterlife memories that shape the character of other Images whom the deceased affected. The belief in immortality suggests an analogy with the principle of the conservation of energy in physics. In physics, the total energy of an isolated system remains constant. Whatever internal changes may take place, energy disappears in one form and reappears in another. Similarly, spiritual energy does not disappear at death. It is transformed. What is remembered of the character and ideals of the deceased affects our way of thinking, feeling, and relating. There are resonances of a life lived and echoes of a voice that reverberate intergenerationally. Memory is not a passive retention of the past. Memory energizes our life and offers testimony to the immortality of influence. We are not alone, not even after death. Our immortality depends on the Image being remembered by others.

Belief in life after death does not deny the sting of death. Nor does belief in life after death necessarily entail belief in another place, or in another world. The Mourner's *Kaddish* makes no reference to another world. It refers to the world that is to be perfected and sanctified in God's name "during the days of your life and during the life of all the house of Israel." Strikingly, in the Mourner's *Kaddish* prayer there is not even a reference to death. The emphasis is on life, this place and this world. Life after death is a belief to be realized by those who, in living on, keep memory alive. Immortality is not merely believed as theory, it is behaved in practice. Life after death is in our hands in life. Whom we have influenced, influence others. The conservation of spiritual energy stored in memory has its enduring afterlife on earth.

Harold M. Schulweis, *Finding Each Other in Judaism: Meditations on the Rites of Passage from Birth to Immortality* (New York: UAHC Press, 2001), 96–97

CHAPTER TWO

ב:א אָמַרְתִּי אֲנִי בְּלִבִּי לְכָה־נָּא אֲנַסְּכָה בְשִׂמְחָה וּרְאֵה בְטוֹב וְהִנֵּה
גַם־הוּא הָבֶל:

2:1 I SAID TO MYSELF, "LET ME INFUSE YOU WITH JOY.
ENJOY GOOD." BUT I FOUND THAT TOO WAS USELESS."

Kohelet's first project in his survey was wisdom. He next turns his attention to the things that give us pleasure. Everything ended up as *hevel* (useless, emptiness, wind). There is no lasting value. How long before even a good meal and the routine pleasures of the flesh become meaningless and without pleasure? The word *anaschah* is difficult to translate. Rashi claims that it is derived from the root *nasach* (to devote as a drink offering). According to the Septuagint and the modern scholar Robert Gordis, the word is derived from the root *nasa* (to test) with the objective suffix *cha* (you). We have followed Rashi and have taken the word to mean "infuse" as an idiom in the context of the statement. However it is translated, the sense of the verse seems to remain the same. Neither joy nor good is sufficient to raise the writer from his melancholy. Rashi explains that away by prophetic means: Solomon knew that unrestricted revelry led to disaster. Perhaps Belshazzar's feast (Daniel 5) is proof of that.

ב:ב לִשְׂחוֹק אָמַרְתִּי מְהוֹלָל וּלְשִׂמְחָה מַה־זֹּה עֹשָׂה:

2:2 OF LAUGHTER, I SAID, "IT'S CRAZY." OF JOY, [I SAID,]
"WHAT DOES IT DO?"

Rashi says that laughter will ultimately be mixed with tears and joy will end in sorrow. Kohelet seems unable to enjoy the moment. He fails to recognize that life is made up of separate moments. Pleasure may have no lasting value, but life itself does not last forever either. Perhaps Kohelet reflects the perspective of those who are comparatively well off, have their basic needs met, and can ponder the value of the pleasures that are readily available to them. Those who rarely have the opportunity for laughter or joy would not so easily dismiss them.

בּ:ג תַּרְתִּי בְלִבִּי לִמְשׁוֹךְ בַּיַּיִן אֶת־בְּשָׂרִי וְלִבִּי נֹהֵג בַּחָכְמָה וְלֶאֱחֹז בְּסִכְלוּת עַד אֲשֶׁר־אֶרְאֶה אֵי־זֶה טוֹב לִבְנֵי הָאָדָם אֲשֶׁר יַעֲשׂוּ תַּחַת הַשָּׁמַיִם מִסְפַּר יְמֵי חַיֵּיהֶם:

2:3 I EXPERIMENTED GIVING MY BODY OVER TO WINE AND GRABBING HOLD OF FOLLY, BUT MY MIND OPERATED WITH WISDOM AND I COULD SEE WHAT WAS GOOD FOR PEOPLE TO DO IN THE NUMBER OF DAYS BENEATH THE SUN.

Which of the two, good wine or wisdom, is preferable? Kohelet lined them up for evaluation. He increased his possessions. He achieved all of the pleasures available to humans. In everything that he did, he outdid everyone who had lived before him in Jerusalem. He did it all while still maintaining his pursuit, his search for wisdom. This is a difficult verse to translate. The author uses common words in uncommon ways. *Tarti v'libi* (literally, "I explored in my mind") is translated as "I experimented." *Limshoch* (to pull, attract, stretch) is oddly joined in this verse with *bayayin* (with wine) and *b'sari* (my flesh, my body). Some critical scholars emend this verse on the basis of Song of Songs 2:5, changing *limshoch* to *lismoch* (sustain). The clause *v'libi noheig bachochmah* (but my mind operated with wisdom) seems out of place. If the Masoretic text is maintained, then *v'libi* should be understood as "though my heart" or "but my heart," which suggests a sharp contrast with *b'sari* (my flesh). Rashi makes the same contrast. Ibn Ezra comments that the author attempted to join the two after concluding that wisdom brought pain and joy had no benefit at all.

בּ:ד הִגְדַּלְתִּי מַעֲשָׂי בָּנִיתִי לִי בָּתִּים נָטַעְתִּי לִי כְּרָמִים:

2:4 I INCREASED MY POSSESSIONS. I BUILT HOUSES AND PLANTED VINEYARDS FOR MYSELF.

The first clause, "I increased my possessions," follows Ibn Ezra's understanding of *higdalti maasai*. The *Targum* gives a charming reason why vineyards were planted: not only so that Solomon might have wine but also so that the heads of the Sanhedrin might share it. The suggestion that Kohelet built more than one house and planted more than one vineyard is a reflection of his wealth and his penchant for spending. He denied nothing for himself, but what did he have?

בּ:ה עָשִׂיתִי לִי גַּנּוֹת וּפַרְדֵּסִים וְנָטַעְתִּי בָהֶם עֵץ כָּל־פֶּרִי:

2:5 I LAID OUT GARDENS AND PARKS, AND I PLANTED EVERY KIND OF FRUIT TREE IN THEM.

Pardeisim (parks; singular, *pardeis*) is taken from Persian to mean "pleasure garden"; it underlies the English word "paradise." Kohelet's use of land for pleasure (rather than to grow food) is another indicator of his wealth, as is the notion that he planted *every* kind of fruit. The *Targum* explains that the gardens grew three kinds of spices: one kind for food, one kind for wine, and one kind for medicine. Rashi imagines that Kohelet did not have to roam the world—or even have others do the roaming for him—to gather the various kinds of fruit. As the master of all knowledge, including the sciences of agriculture and geology, Kohelet knew that there were subterranean channels that crisscrossed the earth and ended in Jerusalem. Instead of having to travel to a specific area where a particular fruit was grown, Kohelet planted that fruit on the channel coming from that area as it emerged in Jerusalem. Thus, he could grow peppers in Jerusalem that were indigenous to Ethiopia. If possessions were everything, then Kohelet had everything.

עָשִׂיתִי לִי בְּרֵכוֹת מָיִם לְהַשְׁקוֹת מֵהֶם יַעַר צוֹמֵחַ עֵצִים: ב:ו

2:6 I HAD POOLS OF WATER DUG TO IRRIGATE A FOREST GROWING TREES.

Rashi explains that the pools had another use: fish were raised in them. For Ibn Ezra, the trees of this verse were not fruit-bearing. Whatever the exact meaning, it appears that each verse describes an increase in Kohelet's wealth.

קָנִיתִי עֲבָדִים וּשְׁפָחוֹת וּבְנֵי־בַיִת הָיָה לִי גַּם מִקְנֶה בָקָר וָצֹאן ב:ז
הַרְבֵּה הָיָה לִי מִכֹּל שֶׁהָיוּ לְפָנַי בִּירוּשָׁלָם:

2:7 I PURCHASED MALE AND FEMALE SLAVES, ALTHOUGH I ALREADY HAD A HOUSEHOLD STAFF. I HAD MORE FLOCKS OF CATTLE AND HERDS OF SHEEP THAN ANYBODY BEFORE ME IN JERUSALEM.

After recounting his real property, Kohelet now recounts some of his movable property. In the following verse, he recounts even more.

כָּנַסְתִּי לִי גַּם־כֶּסֶף וְזָהָב וּסְגֻלַּת מְלָכִים וְהַמְּדִינוֹת עָשִׂיתִי לִי ב:ח
שָׁרִים וְשָׁרוֹת וְתַעֲנֻגוֹת בְּנֵי הָאָדָם שִׁדָּה וְשִׁדּוֹת:

2:8 I AMASSED FOR MYSELF SILVER AND GOLD AND THE TREASURES OF KINGS AND PROVINCES. I ACQUIRED MALE AND FEMALE SINGERS, AND ALL MANNER OF HUMAN DELIGHTS, AS WELL AS VARIOUS CONCUBINES.

The last two words, *shidah v'shidot*, are translated in various ways. Rashi provides two different translations. He suggests that the phrase means either "ornamented chariots" or, following talmudic usage (cf. *Gittin* 68a), "boxes." Ibn Ezra notes the sexual connotation of *taanugot b'nei haadam* (human delights) and translates the *shidah v'shidot* as "women." He derives the word *shidah* from *shadad* (to rape or ravage). We have translated the two words as "various concubines," reflecting both the singular and plural forms as reflected in the Hebrew.

ב:ט וְגָדַלְתִּי וְהוֹסַפְתִּי מִכֹּל שֶׁהָיָה לְפָנַי בִּירוּשָׁלָ͏ִם אַף חָכְמָתִי עָמְדָה לִּי:

2:9 THUS, I WAS RICHER THAN ANYONE WHO HAD EVER BEEN IN JERUSALEM. EVEN SO, MY WISDOM STAYED WITH ME.

The writer invites the question: If "wisdom stayed," why did Kohelet continue to amass wealth of so many different kinds? What was the prize for all this wealth? Whatever kind of wealth he acquired, he would still not be able to take it with him.

ב:י וְכֹל אֲשֶׁר שָׁאֲלוּ עֵינַי לֹא אָצַלְתִּי מֵהֶם לֹא־מָנַעְתִּי אֶת־לִבִּי מִכָּל־שִׂמְחָה כִּי־לִבִּי שָׂמֵחַ מִכָּל־עֲמָלִי וְזֶה־הָיָה חֶלְקִי מִכָּל־עֲמָלִי:

2:10 I WITHHELD NOTHING [FROM MYSELF] THAT MY EYES SOUGHT. I DENIED MYSELF NO PLEASURE. FOR I GOT ENJOYMENT FROM MY WEALTH. BUT THAT WAS ALL I GOT OUT OF MY LABOR.

In anticipation of a more modern sentiment, Kohelet worked hard so that he could play hard. That was the reward. Like so many, he seems to have convinced himself that he has it all. Yet, his need to recount his wealth is an indication that he has his doubts after all.

ב:יא וּפָנִיתִי אֲנִי בְּכָל־מַעֲשַׂי שֶׁעָשׂוּ יָדַי וּבֶעָמָל שֶׁעָמַלְתִּי לַעֲשׂוֹת וְהִנֵּה הַכֹּל הֶבֶל וּרְעוּת רוּחַ וְאֵין יִתְרוֹן תַּחַת הַשָּׁמֶשׁ:

2:11 THEN I TURNED MY THOUGHTS TO ALL THAT I HAD GOTTEN, ALL THAT I HAD WORKED FOR. BUT IT WAS ALL USELESS, A STRIVING AFTER WIND. THERE IS NO [LASTING] VALUE UNDER THE SUN.

Our translation of "I turned my thoughts" (or "I reflected") follows Ibn Ezra's translation of *ufaniti* (literally, "and I turned,") as "and my heart saw." Kohelet denied himself nothing. He was delighted with all the enrichment he received for his toil.

But that was all he received for all his work. The uncertain nature of human life and the unstable quality of human possessions moved the writer to declare that everything is *hevel* (useless, emptiness). There is no net gain for all his work. Who knows what the future will bring?

ב:יב וּפָנִיתִי אֲנִי לִרְאוֹת חָכְמָה וְהוֹלֵלוֹת וְסִכְלוּת כִּי מֶה הָאָדָם שֶׁיָּבוֹא אַחֲרֵי הַמֶּלֶךְ אֵת אֲשֶׁר־כְּבָר עָשׂוּהוּ:

2:12 MY THOUGHTS TURNED [ONCE AGAIN] TO APPRAISING WISDOM, MADNESS, AND FOLLY, [THINKING,] WHAT WILL THE PERSON BE LIKE WHO COMES AFTER THE RULER HAS ALREADY ACTED?

Who or what is the "ruler" determines the real meaning of the verse. For the *Targum* and for Rashi, the ruler is God. Therefore, the verse asks what benefit prayer can have once God has acted to condemn that person. For Ibn Ezra, there are two possibilities. Perhaps the ruler is God and the verse is a statement of awe. What can a human do, seeing what God has already done? Alternatively, on the basis of Nehemiah 5:7, the word *hamelech* is not translated as "ruler." Rather, it is the verb *himaleich*—which requires a change in vowels—"to take counsel." Thus, the verse is a statement of wisdom. What is the point of taking counsel after something has already happened? Some modern scholars, like Robert Gordis (*Koheleth,* p. 211), take *hamelech* as "ruler" but refer it to the author who presents himself as Kohelet, "king in Jerusalem." With this in mind, the verse would ask the question: What is the point of doing something that the king has already done? Other scholars also take *hamelech* as a reference to Kohelet, who reasoned, "Someone will succeed me and receive all that for which I worked. And I don't even know what that person will be like. But I do know that he or she did not work for it, and I will therefore not benefit from my own work." The author knows what we know: you can't take any of it with you to the grave.

ב:יג וְרָאִיתִי אָנִי שֶׁיֵּשׁ יִתְרוֹן לַחָכְמָה מִן־הַסִּכְלוּת כִּיתְרוֹן הָאוֹר מִן־הַחֹשֶׁךְ:

2:13 I SAW THAT THERE IS A VALUE TO WISDOM OVER FOOLISHNESS, JUST AS THERE IS A VALUE OF LIGHT OVER DARKNESS.

This verse and the one that follows seem to contradict the previous sentiments of the author. Some modern scholars suggest that these are two proverbs that Kohelet quotes so that he can refute them. Others may argue that Kohelet's own perspective has changed as he has grown older. Thus, the older Kohelet refutes the thoughts he had as a younger man. The *Targum* has Solomon accept the plain meaning of these two verses as a result of prophecy. In other words, these verses will be his ultimate conclusion after he finishes writing the book. It appears that those who pursued the purposes of the Enlightenment built their world based on the acceptance of the notion of this verse.

ב:יד הֶחָכָם עֵינָיו בְּרֹאשׁוֹ וְהַכְּסִיל בַּחֹשֶׁךְ הוֹלֵךְ וְיָדַעְתִּי גַם־אָנִי שֶׁמִּקְרֶה אֶחָד יִקְרֶה אֶת־כֻּלָּם:

2:14 THE WISE PERSON HAS EYES IN HIS [OR HER] HEAD. THE FOOL PROCEEDS IN DARKNESS. BUT I KNEW THAT THE SAME FATE AWAITS EVERYONE.

So he concluded, "There is a value of wisdom over idiocy, just as there is a value of light over darkness." The wise individual avoids pitfalls. Nevertheless, in the last analysis, everyone dies. The fool has the same fate as the one who is wise: death. Rashi, following the *Targum,* points out that "the wise person," at least, can anticipate the future better than the fool. One can conclude that the nature of wisdom is to understand the process of nature and history so that one can direct one's life in a better manner.

ב:טו וְאָמַרְתִּי אֲנִי בְּלִבִּי כְּמִקְרֵה הַכְּסִיל גַּם־אֲנִי יִקְרֵנִי וְלָמָּה חָכַמְתִּי אֲנִי אָז יוֹתֵר וְדִבַּרְתִּי בְלִבִּי שֶׁגַּם־זֶה הָבֶל:

2:15 SO I SAID TO MYSELF, "IF WHAT IS GOING TO HAPPEN TO THE FOOL WILL ALSO HAPPEN TO ME, WHAT ADVANTAGE HAS BEEN MY WISDOM?" I THOUGHT TO MYSELF, THAT TOO WAS EMPTY.

The *Targum* understands Kohelet, as Solomon, to say that Saul was the fool who lost his kingdom, because he failed to take the revenge on Amalek by killing Magog that God mandated. Saul thinks to himself, "I might lose mine by becoming too wise in matters other than the word of *Adonai*." Rashi reads the verse as an expression of Kohelet's wondering why he should attempt to be righteous if both the wise person and the fool die. In different ways, the *Targum* and Rashi both echo Kohelet's sense of uncertainty of life. Virtue, therefore, cannot be based on the anticipation of a reward.

ב:טז כִּי אֵין זִכְרוֹן לֶחָכָם עִם־הַכְּסִיל לְעוֹלָם בְּשֶׁכְּבָר הַיָּמִים הַבָּאִים הַכֹּל נִשְׁכָּח וְאֵיךְ יָמוּת הֶחָכָם עִם־הַכְּסִיל:

2:16 THERE IS NO PERMANENT MEMORIAL FOR THE WISE PERSON OR FOR THE FOOL. AS THE DAYS GO BY, ALL ARE FORGOTTEN. THE WISE PERSON DIES, JUST AS DOES THE FOOL.

It seems that there is no advantage to wisdom. Neither wisdom nor folly enables one to leave a trace. Everything ends up in oblivion. It is sad that the wise person dies that way. As a result, life itself becomes distasteful. In the sight of a common fate, what is the use of any of it?

ב:יז וְשָׂנֵאתִי אֶת־הַחַיִּים כִּי רַע עָלַי הַמַּעֲשֶׂה שֶׁנַּעֲשָׂה תַּחַת הַשָּׁמֶשׁ כִּי־הַכֹּל הֶבֶל וּרְעוּת רוּחַ:

2:17 SO I DESPISED LIFE. EVERYTHING THAT TAKES PLACE BENEATH THE SUN DISTRESSED ME. IT IS ALL EMPTINESS AND THE PURSUIT OF WIND.

The *Targum* softens Kohelet's expression of the pain of life by noting that this is just how it is in this life. Rashi, however, understands the verse as Solomon's prophecy as to what happened during Rehoboam's reign. Ibn Ezra looks closely at the language, pointing out that the word *chayim* can be the adjective "alive," as in Deuteronomy 4:4, or it can be the noun "life," as in Deuteronomy 30:19. He thinks that it is being used in this verse as an adjective: "I hate those who alive...."

ב:יח וְשָׂנֵאתִי אֲנִי אֶת־כָּל־עֲמָלִי שֶׁאֲנִי עָמֵל תַּחַת הַשָּׁמֶשׁ שֶׁאַנִּיחֶנּוּ לָאָדָם שֶׁיִּהְיֶה אַחֲרָי:

2:18 AND I DESPISED ALL THAT I HAD LABORED FOR AND GAINED UNDER THE SUN, AS I WILL LEAVE IT FOR THE PERSON WHO COMES AFTER ME.

Wealth becomes a taunt because we can't take it with us. What will I do even with the legacy of my understanding of life? Even the wisdom gained throughout life is transitory. Now, contemplating his old age—and the end of his life—he begrudges the person who will succeed him. As if it would make a difference when he is dead, he continues his questioning in the next verse.

ב:יט וּמִי יוֹדֵעַ הֶחָכָם יִהְיֶה אוֹ סָכָל וְיִשְׁלַט בְּכָל־עֲמָלִי שֶׁעָמַלְתִּי וְשֶׁחָכַמְתִּי תַּחַת הַשָּׁמֶשׁ גַּם־זֶה הָבֶל:

2:19 WHO KNOWS WHETHER THAT PERSON WILL BE WISE OR FOOLISH? THAT PERSON WILL CONTROL ALL THE WEALTH THAT I SO CLEVERLY AMASSED BENEATH THE SUN. THIS TOO IS USELESS.

One thing is certain: wise or foolish, the inheritor of Kohelet's wealth will be alive when Kohelet is dead. Perhaps Kohelet is worried more about his mortality and its relevant problems than about his loss of wealth.

ב:כ וְסַבּוֹתִי אֲנִי לְיַאֵשׁ אֶת־לִבִּי עַל כָּל־הֶעָמָל שֶׁעָמַלְתִּי תַּחַת הַשָּׁמֶשׁ:

2:20 REFLECTING ON ALL THE WEALTH THAT I HAD AMASSED BENEATH THE SUN, I DESPAIRED.

Kohelet's despair is a reflection of his values. If wealth is his goal, then despair must follow, since greed is infinite. If power is his ultimate concern, then despair must follow, since no one can overpower death. We have to wait until the end of the book before we can decide whether Kohelet possessed true wisdom. If he did, he would have known what to value. No one can be saved from grief, but some can be saved from despair.

ב:כא כִּי־יֵשׁ אָדָם שֶׁעֲמָלוֹ בְּחָכְמָה וּבְדַעַת וּבְכִשְׁרוֹן וּלְאָדָם שֶׁלֹּא עָמַל־בּוֹ יִתְּנֶנּוּ חֶלְקוֹ גַּם־זֶה הֶבֶל וְרָעָה רַבָּה:

2:21 SOMEONE WHO MAY HAVE AMASSED WEALTH USING WISDOM, KNOWLEDGE, AND SKILL MUST END UP SHARING IT WITH SOMEONE WHO NEVER WORKED FOR IT. THIS TOO IS USELESS AND A GREAT EVIL.

Again, Kohelet worries about what will happen to his wealth once he is gone and who will get it. What might be understood from this is that he did not have children, lacked a family, and had no friends. It seems that there was no one to whom he could leave his possessions and feel that somebody he knew, somebody he cared for, would benefit from the wealth that he left. To be rich and yet to be so poor!

ב:כב כִּי מֶה־הֹוֶה לָאָדָם בְּכָל־עֲמָלוֹ וּבְרַעְיוֹן לִבּוֹ שֶׁהוּא עָמֵל תַּחַת הַשָּׁמֶשׁ:

2:22 WHAT DO YOU GET FOR ALL THE WORK AND WORRY,
FOR ALL THAT YOU DO BENEATH THE SUN?

We follow Rashi's understanding of *rayon* (thought) as *d'agah* (worry). It seems that Kohelet didn't even enjoy amassing his wealth and working out his plans for his own lifetime. He seemed to find no pleasure in anything. Kohelet suffered in leaving his money behind as well as in making it.

ב:כג כִּי כָל־יָמָיו מַכְאֹבִים וָכַעַס עִנְיָנוֹ גַּם־בַּלַּיְלָה לֹא־שָׁכַב לִבּוֹ גַּם־זֶה הֶבֶל הוּא:

2:23 EVERY DAY HURTS. EACH ONE IS FILLED WITH GRIEF.
EVEN AT NIGHT, YOUR MIND CAN'T GET REST. THIS
TOO IS USELESS.

We follow Rashi, who understands *inyano* (literally, "its matter") as referring to each day and interprets it as *minhago* (its customary quality). Ibn Ezra suggests that the reason Kohelet is troubled day and night is that he keeps thinking about failed plans by day and dreams about them at night. This is too useless, because the past can't be brought back, no matter how much wealth one has, and because in this view money ultimately doesn't matter.

ב:כד אֵין־טוֹב בָּאָדָם שֶׁיֹּאכַל וְשָׁתָה וְהֶרְאָה אֶת־נַפְשׁוֹ טוֹב בַּעֲמָלוֹ גַּם־זֹה רָאִיתִי אָנִי כִּי מִיַּד הָאֱלֹהִים הִיא:

2:24 THERE IS NOTHING BETTER TO DO THAN TO EAT AND
DRINK, AND ENJOY ALL YOU HAVE. I KNOW EVEN THAT
COMES FROM GOD.

Now it seems that Kohelet has changed his mind. Perhaps troubled by this change, Rashi interprets this verse as a question. Ibn Ezra, however, takes the verse as a positive statement in praise of the two things that Kohelet found worthy of praise: eating and drinking. Perhaps it is not surprising that Kohelet changed his mind. We all make up our minds and then change them, only to make them up again and then change them once more. That is simply a part of being human.

ב:כה כִּי מִי יֹאכַל וּמִי יָחוּשׁ חוּץ מִמֶּנִּי:

2:25 WHO ELSE BUT ME WILL BE EATING AND ENJOYING?

Yachush (enjoying) is a problematic word. The *Targum* relates it to *chashasha* (fear, anxiety). Ibn Ezra takes the word to mean "to haste." Some modern scholars follow the *Targum* and interpret the word to mean "abstain." Others take the word to mean "sense" or "enjoy," as we have done.

ב:כו כִּי לְאָדָם שֶׁטּוֹב לְפָנָיו נָתַן חָכְמָה וְדַעַת וְשִׂמְחָה וְלַחוֹטֶא נָתַן עִנְיָן לֶאֱסוֹף וְלִכְנוֹס לָתֵת לְטוֹב לִפְנֵי הָאֱלֹהִים גַּם־זֶה הֶבֶל וּרְעוּת רוּחַ:

2:26 WISDOM, KNOWLEDGE, AND JOY ARE GIVEN TO THE ONE GOD FAVORS. TO THE ONE GOD DOES NOT [FAVOR], GOD GIVES THE ANGUISH OF GAINING AND GETTING—AND GIVING AWAY TO SOMEONE ELSE WHOM GOD DOES FAVOR. THIS TOO IS USELESS AND CHASING AFTER WIND.

This is a problematic verse. Perhaps Kohelet changed his mind once again. Maybe this is a gloss added by a pious editor. Who is the *choteh* (literally, "sinner"), the one who is not favored by God? The *Targum* places the "joy" of the person in the world-to-come in order to guarantee the "truth" of the verse. The *choteh* of the verse is translated by the *Targum* as *gavrah chayah* (guilty person). In his commentary, Robert Gordis points out that *choteh* can mean "one out of favor," as in I Kings 1:21. Rashi translates *inyan* (matter) as *minhag d'agah* (custom of worry), which we have translated as "anguish." In reviewing his life in this verse Kohelet seems to have reverted to his earlier complaint: wealth is an albatross around his neck. No matter what he has made, he has to give it away when he dies.

Belshazzar

Belshazzar (literally, "Bel protect the king!") was the last of the kings of Babylon (Daniel 5:1) and the son of Nabonidus by Nitocris, who was the daughter of Nebuchadnezzar and the widow of Nergal-sharezer. He made a great feast to a thousand of his lords while he was still young. When filled with wine, he sent for the sacred vessels his "father" (Daniel 5:2), or grandfather, Nebuchadnezzar had carried away from the Temple in Jerusalem, so that he and his princes could drink out of them. In the midst of their party, the king saw a hand tracing the announcement of God's judgment on the wall. This is the source of the idiom "the writing on the wall." That night, such a judgment fell upon him. At the insistence of the queen (i.e., his mother), Daniel was brought in, and he interpreted the writing. That same night the kingdom of the Chaldeans came to an end, and the king was slain (Daniel 5:30).

Enlightenment

Enlightenment (also called the Haskalah in a Jewish context) was the philosophical movement of the eighteenth century that stressed rationalism and the rejection of traditional, social, political, and religious notions. The Enlightenment affected all religions, including the Jewish community, first in Western Europe and then in Eastern Europe. In Western Europe, the impact of the new ideas of the Enlightenment upon the Jewish community led to modern Judaism in all its forms; in Eastern Europe, those new ideas also led to secularism, socialism, and Zionism.

The World-to-Come

The eschatological concept of a world-to-come *(olam haba)* developed during the period of the Second Temple. This concept was expanded upon in the subsequent rabbinic literature. While the term *olam* originally was related to space, it later took on the dimension of time. Jewish tradition suggests that a major event, such as the Day of Judgment, would bring this world to an end and usher in the next world, that is, the world-to-come. "Heaven" and "paradise" are terms used interchangeably to define *olam haba.* However, some make a distinction between the temporary place where souls reside prior to final judgment and the "other world" where the departed souls of "good" people permanently reside.

Sanhedrin

While the apparent form of the Sanhedrin may have changed over the course of its existence, it was primarily a legislative body that dealt with religious matters. On rare occasions, it acted as a court. It probably existed in the Land of Israel during the Roman period—before and after the destruction of the Temple—until approximately 425 C.E. Hellenistic sources describe the Sanhedrin as a political body of seventy-one judges, led by the High Priest. Rabbinic sources describe it as composed of scholars, led by the *nasi* and the *av beit din,* the leaders of the Pharisees.

GLEANINGS

Ritual and Spirituality

A ritual is a spiritual ballet. It captures in symbols the emotions that go with an important life transition. Think of the cheer that goes up when the glass is broken at the wedding, or at the moment of finality when the mourner shovels dirt onto the coffin at a funeral. Passing from one stage of life to another can be frightening; rituals ease the transition by affirming the sacredness of the moment and helping people feel a connection to their community and heritage.

Judy Petsonk, *Taking Judaism Personally: Creating a Meaningful Spiritual Life*
(New York: Free Press, 1996), 142

"Heaven and Hell Can Both Be Had in This World"
 (Yiddish Proverb)

Our very humanness means we sometimes behave badly. Out teachers cared mightily that we live up to the high standards set by Jewish law and communal ideals. They couldn't easily rationalize how little good most of us actually do and how easily and regularly we fall into sin. Yet despite their unblinking look at how we actually behave, the rabbis remained optimistic, knowing that the Torah's positive influence upon our moral choices cannot be disputed: "I have put before you life and death, blessing and curse. Choose life—that you and your descendants may live!" (Deut. 30:19). They attributed our chronic sinning to the powerful nature of the evil urge, a foe so wily and untiring that it can never be permanently defeated. Nonetheless, the Torah's teaching is plain: with God's help we can ally ourselves with God's goodness and rule humanity's evil streak. One of our sages actually pictured us as schizoid, with the two *yetzarim* evenly split in their ability to dictate our actions: "As R. Levi taught: There are six parts of the body that serve a person; three are under his control and three are not. The eyes, the ears, and the nose are not under a person's control; he sees what he doesn't want to see, hears what he doesn't want to hear, and smells what he doesn't want to smell. The mouth, the hand, and the foot are under a person's control. If he wants he can use his mouth to study Torah or speak gossip and blasphemy. He can use his hand to give charity or steal and kill. He can use his feet to walk to synagogue or houses of study, or to brothels" (Genesis *Rabbah* 67:3).

Eugene B. Borowitz and Frances Weinman Schwartz, The Jewish Moral Virtues
(Philadelphia: The Jewish Publication Society, 1999), 175–76

Success

When success becomes an end in itself, it is unlikely that it can serve as a means to happiness—or to anything else. Even if success can serve as an ingredient in happiness, it is only one of many ingredients needed. And if success has been purchased at the price of having sacrificed all the other elements, enduring happiness will continue to elude us. Furthermore, ... what is true of success is also true of the acquisition of money. When it begins as a means to an end and then becomes an end in itself, the original goal grows ever more elusive. Just as having more success does not guarantee being happier, having more money is no guarantor of increased happiness.

Byron L. Sherwin, Why Be Good? Seeking Our Best Selves in a Challenging World
(New York: Daybreak Books, 1998), 176

Laughter

There can be joy in silence or with tears, just as there can be laughter in terror or in pain. When people are joyous, they are at their best: they are generous, kind, grateful, and reverent. Happy families are just that; if they don't actually laugh, they smile a lot. They laugh at jokes, the state of the universe, and, above all, they laugh at themselves. I am not talking here about ridicule or jest, nor laughter from embarrassment or anxiety. It is a joy to be alive.

I'm talking about learning how to discern the humor in even our "holiest" undertakings. If by the word "sacred" we mean that we cannot laugh at it, then it is less than sacred. But conversely whatever occasions joyous laughter turns out to be sacred.

Lawrence Kushner, *The Book of Words: Talking Spiritual Life, Living Spiritual Talk*
(Woodstock, Vt.: Jewish Lights Publishing, 1995), 63

CHAPTER THREE

ג:א לַכֹּל זְמָן וְעֵת לְכָל־חֵפֶץ תַּחַת הַשָּׁמָיִם:

3:1 EVERYTHING HAS ITS MOMENT. THERE IS A TIME FOR
EVERYTHING BENEATH THE HEAVENS.

The *Targum* takes the first clause to refer to a person and translates *l'chol gevar yaytay
zimna* as "to every person comes a time." The Aramaic suggests the nuance of
"opportunity" in its translation of the Hebrew term *z'man* (time). Thus, we have
translated the Hebrew as "moment."

ג:ב עֵת לָלֶדֶת וְעֵת לָמוּת עֵת לָטַעַת וְעֵת לַעֲקוֹר נָטוּעַ:

3:2 A TIME TO BE BORN AND A TIME TO DIE. A TIME TO
PLANT AND A TIME TO UPROOT WHAT HAS BEEN
PLANTED.

Ibn Ezra gives two explanations of the "times" given. According to philosophers, there
are specifically beneficial times for all these events to occur, while the astrologers
believed in beneficial configurations of the constellations. It is not clear whether any
kind of specific time is intended in the verse. Perhaps the writer is indicating that the
drama of human life is played out on a stage of time. We measure change on that
stage. We control some changes; we cannot control others. We are born, as the
Rabbis said (in *Pirkei Avot* 4:29), against our wills, and we die against our wills. What
we do with our lives is up to us. In dealing with the first verse, Rashi refers the last
clause to nations and peoples.

ג:ג עֵת לַהֲרוֹג וְעֵת לִרְפּוֹא עֵת לִפְרוֹץ וְעֵת לִבְנוֹת:

3:3 A TIME TO KILL AND A TIME TO HEAL. A TIME TO TEAR
DOWN AND A TIME TO BUILD UP.

The *Targum* understands the first clause as "there is an opportune time to kill in
battle, and there is an opportune time to heal someone who is gravely ill."
Rashi takes the verse to refer to aspects of history in which different ruling peoples
rose and fell.

ג:ד עֵת לִבְכּוֹת וְעֵת לִשְׂחוֹק עֵת סְפוֹד וְעֵת רְקוֹד:

3:4 A TIME TO WEEP AND A TIME TO LAUGH. A TIME OF
MOURNING AND A TIME OF DANCING.

As might be expected, Rashi understands the first part of the first clause to refer to
Tishah B'Av and the second part to the world-to-come. He understands the second
clause as referring to individual human events: funerals and weddings.

ג:ה עֵת לְהַשְׁלִיךְ אֲבָנִים וְעֵת כְּנוֹס אֲבָנִים עֵת לַחֲבוֹק וְעֵת לִרְחֹק
מֵחַבֵּק:

3:5 A TIME TO THROW STONES AND A TIME TO GATHER
STONES. A TIME TO EMBRACE AND A TIME TO AVOID
EMBRACING.

The *Targum* understands "embrace" to mean "embracing a woman" and "avoid
embracing" as "abstaining," like during the shivah period (of seven days of
mourning). Given the association of meaning of the *Targum* and the pairing of the two
clauses, it was commonly assumed that the first clause had the same sexual
connotation as the second. Thus, the midrash (in *Kohelet Rabbah* 3:6) takes "the time
to throw stones" as a reference to when a woman is "ritually pure" (with regard to
the laws of *nidah*, dealing with menstruation) and the "time to gather stones" when a
woman is "ritually impure," when sexual activity is prohibited. Some modern scholars
have accepted this explanation of the second clause. Basing his explanation on
Lamentations 4:1, Rashi understands the "stones" that were cast off as those young
men who were slaughtered after the fall of Jerusalem. Rashi based his explanation of
"gathered stones" on Zechariah 9:16, suggesting that these were the young men who
returned from exile.

ג:ו עֵת לְבַקֵּשׁ וְעֵת לְאַבֵּד עֵת לִשְׁמוֹר וְעֵת לְהַשְׁלִיךְ:

3:6 THERE IS A TIME TO SEEK AND A TIME TO LOSE, A TIME
TO KEEP AND A TIME TO CAST OFF.

In the context of this verse, the *Targum* takes property as that which is sought and
that which is lost. It takes merchandise as what is to be either safeguarded or cast
into the sea in the face of a storm. Rashi reads the verse differently, taking the
dispersed of the people of Israel as those who are sought and those who have been
lost among the nations.

ג:ז עֵת לִקְרוֹעַ וְעֵת לִתְפּוֹר עֵת לַחֲשׁוֹת וְעֵת לְדַבֵּר:

3:7 THERE IS A TIME FOR RIPPING AND A TIME FOR
SEWING. THERE IS A TIME TO BE SILENT AND A TIME
TO SPEAK.

The *Targum* refers to the "ripping" as what is done as a sign of mourning, what is called "cutting *k'riah*." Perhaps the entire verse is directed to those practices related to mourning, both to the mourners and those who attempt to comfort those who are bereaved. Knowing when to speak to a mourner and when to be silent is extremely important. Rashi understands the first clause as relating to the loss of the Davidic kingdom and its ultimate restoration. He takes the second clause as a reference to Aaron's silence (Leviticus 10:3) and Moses' song (Exodus 15:1).

ג:ח עֵת לֶאֱהֹב וְעֵת לִשְׂנֹא עֵת מִלְחָמָה וְעֵת שָׁלוֹם:

3:8 THERE IS A TIME FOR LOVE AND A TIME FOR HATE.
THERE IS A TIME FOR WAR AND A TIME FOR PEACE.

Much of human history has shown that the time for love is short and the time of hate much too long. As for war, it is still an unfortunately attractive means for settling disputes. Peace is the ideal to be hoped for.

ג:ט מַה־יִּתְרוֹן הָעוֹשֶׂה בַּאֲשֶׁר הוּא עָמֵל:

3:9 WHAT GAIN DOES ONE GET WITH ALL OF ONE'S TOIL?

The writer asks that if there are set times in which things occur, what is the point of human effort? If what is going to happen will happen, why bother trying to make things happen at all?

ג:י רָאִיתִי אֶת־הָעִנְיָן אֲשֶׁר נָתַן אֱלֹהִים לִבְנֵי הָאָדָם לַעֲנוֹת בּוֹ:

3:10 I HAVE SEEN THE AFFAIR THAT GOD HAS GIVEN PEOPLE
TO BE CONCERNED WITH.

There are two words that present us with challenges in translation: *inyan* (matter or, as above "affair"), *laanot* (the infinitive of *anah*, "to answer" or "be concerned with"). The sense of the first word in the context of this verse is of "the way things are." Rashi explains the word as *minhag* (customary behavior). The sense of the second word is "to respond to." Rashi explains this word as *l'hitnaheig* (to deal with). Possibly reflecting the meaning of *anah* in what is called the *pi-eil* intensive form (to oppress, abuse, or torture), the *Targum* translates *inyan* as *gavan isurin ufuranuta* (the quality of prohibitions and punishments). The *Targum* translates *laanot* by *l'sagafut-hon* (to suffer) and then specifies the kind of people who deserve that suffering and those punishments: *inun rashiin* (those who are wicked). By looking at its simple meaning, readers can understand Kohelet's comment: I have seen the world as it is, and it is a sorry business.

ג:יא אֶת־הַכֹּל עָשָׂה יָפֶה בְעִתּוֹ גַּם אֶת־הָעֹלָם נָתַן בְּלִבָּם מִבְּלִי אֲשֶׁר לֹא־יִמְצָא הָאָדָם אֶת־הַמַּעֲשֶׂה אֲשֶׁר־עָשָׂה הָאֱלֹהִים מֵרֹאשׁ וְעַד־סוֹף:

3:11 GOD BRINGS EVERYTHING TO PASS PROPERLY IN ITS TIME. GOD HAS PUT ETERNITY IN PEOPLE'S MINDS, YET NOBODY CAN DETERMINE WHAT GOD WILL BRING TO PASS FROM BEGINNING TO END.

By moving the vowels while retaining the consonants, the midrash (*Tanchuma, K'doshim* 8) interprets the word *haolam* as if it were *heelim* (hides). The Rabbis of this midrash explain that God hides from each of us the time when we will die. Thus, we continue to live as if the time of our death were distant from us. Rashi and Ibn Ezra make similar comments on the verse. Rashi says that the written form (what is called the *k'tiv*) of *haolam* suggests *haalamah* (concealment). The day of death is hidden from every human being. If such were not the case, no one would build a house or plant a vineyard. Similarly, Ibn Ezra notes that the "eternity" placed in the human mind means that we operate as if we would live forever. This frustrates Kohelet. Humans can never fully appreciate what God has created: a world in which there is no eternity for us, only for God. Perhaps it is our mortality that goads us to action.

ג:יב יָדַעְתִּי כִּי אֵין טוֹב בָּם כִּי אִם־לִשְׂמוֹחַ וְלַעֲשׂוֹת טוֹב בְּחַיָּיו:

3:12 I KNOW THAT THERE IS NOTHING BETTER THAN TO REJOICE AND DO GOOD IN ONE'S LIFE.

In line with his comment on the preceding verse, Rashi says that since no one knows the day of one's death, one should rejoice in one's lot and do good in the sight of the Creator. Ibn Ezra takes this verse to be directed to those people who have been described in the preceding verses, who spent every waking hour worrying about the deals they made and every night dreaming of their mistakes. Perhaps this verse reflects Kohelet's ambivalence or reflects his own experience. Here he accepts the joys of life, even though he knows that all that he has will ultimately belong to someone else. So Kohelet concludes that we should enjoy ourselves and be decent people, because afterwards, there is nothing.

ג:יג וְגַם כָּל־הָאָדָם שֶׁיֹּאכַל וְשָׁתָה וְרָאָה טוֹב בְּכָל־עֲמָלוֹ מַתַּת אֱלֹהִים הִיא:

3:13 ALSO, IT IS A GIFT OF GOD FOR ANYONE TO EAT, DRINK, AND ENJOY GOOD WITH ONE'S LABORS.

Kohelet now acknowledges that not only is one's life in God's hands but also one's enjoyment of that life. Ibn Ezra takes the verse to indicate that enjoyment itself follows a particular sequence in time, a sequence framed by God.

ג:יד יָדַעְתִּי כִּי כָּל־אֲשֶׁר יַעֲשֶׂה הָאֱלֹהִים הוּא יִהְיֶה לְעוֹלָם עָלָיו אֵין לְהוֹסִיף וּמִמֶּנּוּ אֵין לִגְרֹעַ וְהָאֱלֹהִים עָשָׂה שֶׁיִּרְאוּ מִלְּפָנָיו:

3:14 I KNOW THAT WHATEVER GOD DOES WILL BE FOREVER. ONE CANNOT ADD TO OR TAKE FROM IT. GOD ACTS SO THAT HUMANS SHOULD FEAR GOD.

The *Targum* relates this verse to events in the world that are under God's control. Rashi relates the verse to the physical world, while Ibn Ezra connects the two clauses of the verse: God's unchangeable control of the world is done in order to elicit human awe.

ג:טו מַה־שֶּׁהָיָה כְּבָר הוּא וַאֲשֶׁר לִהְיוֹת כְּבָר הָיָה וְהָאֱלֹהִים יְבַקֵּשׁ אֶת־נִרְדָּף:

3:15 WHAT WAS, WAS ALWAYS THERE. WHAT WILL BE, WAS ALWAYS THERE. AND GOD SEEKS THE PURSUED.

This last clause is problematic. What is the meaning of "God seeks the pursued"? Rashi follows the *Targum* in his explanation, which suggests that God seeks the pursued in order to punish the pursuer. The midrash (*Tanchuma, Emor* 9) suggests that God is on the side of the one pursued *sheafilo tzadik rodef rasha* (even when a righteous person pursues a wicked person). *Nirdaf* is the consequence of action. It may be translated as "disappeared" or "vanished." This allows us to unify the sense of all three clauses. It suggests that God controls all things—things that exist, things that will exist, and things that no longer exist.

ג:טז וְעוֹד רָאִיתִי תַּחַת הַשָּׁמֶשׁ מְקוֹם הַמִּשְׁפָּט שָׁמָּה הָרֶשַׁע וּמְקוֹם הַצֶּדֶק שָׁמָּה הָרָשַׁע:

3:16 THIS TOO HAVE I SEEN BENEATH THE SUN: IN THE PLACE OF JUDGMENT, THERE WAS WICKEDNESS. AND IN THE PLACE OF THE INNOCENT, THERE WAS THE GUILTY.

Kohelet now explores a completely different theme: justice. Since the place of judgment suggests a legal situation, we have read *tzedek* as "innocent" (rather than "righteous") and *rasha* as "guilty" (rather than "wicked"). These emendations require a change of vowels and are supported by the *Targum*, which translates the two words in the second clause as *g'var zakai* (an innocent person) and *gavra chayava* (guilty person). Such a reading is supported by the next verse, as well.

ג:יז אָמַרְתִּי אֲנִי בְּלִבִּי אֶת־הַצַּדִּיק וְאֶת־הָרָשָׁע יִשְׁפֹּט הָאֱלֹהִים כִּי־עֵת לְכָל־חֵפֶץ וְעַל כָּל־הַמַּעֲשֶׂה שָׁם:

3:17 I SAID TO MYSELF, "GOD WILL JUDGE THE INNOCENT AND THE GUILTY, FOR THERE IS A TIME FOR EVERY ACTION THERE."

"There," the last word of the verse, presents us with an obvious problem. Its antedecent is unclear. Where is "there"? According to Rashi, *sham* suggests some future recompense. According to Ibn Ezra, such a recompense will come in the world-to-come. The reader, however, will discover that Kohelet does accept the notion of a world-to-come as the ultimate place of judgment. It is a rabbinic notion that comes later in Jewish theology than does the writing of Kohelet. Some scholars, therefore, have emended *sham* to *sam* (he placed), suggesting that "God has set a time for everything." Other scholars have found such an emendation neither persuasive nor necessary. It may well be that *sham* is used by the author ironically: there may be judgment *there* but not *here*!

ג:יח אָמַרְתִּי אֲנִי בְּלִבִּי עַל־דִּבְרַת בְּנֵי הָאָדָם לְבָרָם הָאֱלֹהִים וְלִרְאוֹת שְׁהֶם־בְּהֵמָה הֵמָּה לָהֶם:

3:18 I SAID TO MYSELF, "WITHOUT REGARD TO PEOPLE, GOD TESTS THEM TO SEE IF INDEED THEY ARE ANIMALS."

This is a difficult verse. *Al divrat* (concerning, because of) occurs here and twice more in Kohelet and in a slightly different form in Psalms (110:4). The *Targum* translates it as *al eisak* as "in the matter of," and Ibn Ezra translates it as *baavur*, "for the sake of." *L'varam* is more difficult. The *Targum* translates the word with two Aramaic words:

l'nasoeihon and *l'mivchaneihon*. Both of these words mean "to test." Ibn Ezra takes the word from *libareiram*, meaning "to inform them." On the basis of I Samuel 17:8, Ibn Ezra takes the word from *barah*, which means "choose." Hence, he concludes "choose them." Rashi takes *lirot* (to see) as *l'harot* (to show). Thus, he suggests "to show that they are animals." The last two words of the verse *heimah lahem* (they are to them) are omitted by some as a repetition (technically referred to as a "dittography") of the word *b'heimah*. Perhaps the English text (since all translations are interpretations) seems clearer than the Hebrew.

גּ:יט כִּי מִקְרֶה בְנֵי־הָאָדָם וּמִקְרֶה הַבְּהֵמָה וּמִקְרֶה אֶחָד לָהֶם כְּמוֹת זֶה כֵּן מוֹת זֶה וְרוּחַ אֶחָד לַכֹּל וּמוֹתַר הָאָדָם מִן־הַבְּהֵמָה אָיִן כִּי הַכֹּל הָבֶל:

3:19 WHAT HAPPENS TO PEOPLE, HAPPENS TO ANIMALS. WHAT HAPPENS IS THE SAME: AS ONE DIES, SO DOES THE OTHER. THE SAME SPIRIT IS IN BOTH. BEING HUMAN HAS NO ADVANTAGE OVER BEING A BEAST. EVERYTHING IS USELESS.

This verse presents a view far different from traditional Jewish belief. Thus, commentators seem to have interpreted its meaning away from the text. The *Targum* explains the common fate of humans and animals as related to those humans who were unrepentant sinners. Ibn Ezra applies the verse to those fools who depend only on what their eyes can see and not on what their minds can understand. It should be noted that for Ibn Ezra, that understanding involves philosophy. The word *ruach* (literally, "wind") carries enough ambiguity that it serves as one of the synonyms for "soul." Hence, it may mean "breath of life." In verse 21, the word refers to what will persist after death. We have chosen to preserve the ambiguity by translating the word as "spirit" in both verses.

גּ:כ הַכֹּל הוֹלֵךְ אֶל־מָקוֹם אֶחָד הַכֹּל הָיָה מִן־הֶעָפָר וְהַכֹּל שָׁב אֶל־הֶעָפָר:

3:20 BOTH GO TO THE SAME PLACE. THEY COME FROM DUST AND RETURN TO DUST.

Death makes all living things equal.

ג:כא מִי יוֹדֵעַ רוּחַ בְּנֵי הָאָדָם הָעֹלָה הִיא לְמָעְלָה וְרוּחַ הַבְּהֵמָה הַיֹּרֶדֶת הִיא לְמַטָּה לָאָרֶץ:

3:21 WHO KNOWS WHETHER THE SPIRIT OF HUMANS RISES UPWARD OR THE SPIRIT OF ANIMALS DESCENDS DOWNWARD TO THE EARTH?

For religions that require reward and punishment to maintain a system of justice, the world-to-come is indispensable. To deny that world is to deny the system. Rashi comments that unlike the spirit of animals, the spirit of humans will have to present an accounting before the Divine Court.

ג:כב וְרָאִיתִי כִּי אֵין טוֹב מֵאֲשֶׁר יִשְׂמַח הָאָדָם בְּמַעֲשָׂיו כִּי־הוּא חֶלְקוֹ כִּי מִי יְבִיאֶנּוּ לִרְאוֹת בְּמֶה שֶׁיִּהְיֶה אַחֲרָיו:

3:22 SO I SAW THAT THERE IS NOTHING BETTER THAN FOR PEOPLE TO REJOICE IN WHAT THEY DO, FOR THAT IS OUR PORTION. WHO CAN ENABLE ONE TO SEE WHAT WILL BE AFTERWARD?

For Rashi, "afterward" is the world-to-come. For Ibn Ezra, this verse presents the view of those who do not believe in that world. It would seem that this verse expresses the this-worldy view of Kohelet that we have seen before and will see again.

Tishah B'Av

Tishah B'Av takes place on the ninth of the Hebrew month of Av, occurring in late summer. It is an observance that primarily marks the destruction of both Temples, as well as other mournful periods of Jewish history, and is referred to as the "black fast." Three other things were to have happened on that day as well: the generation of the desert were told that they would not enter Canaan and would die in the desert, Bar Kochba's fortress was captured by the Romans, and the city of Jerusalem was plowed under and rendered uninhabitable. According to at least one midrash (*B'reishit Rabbah* 19:9), by employing a bit of wordplay, the primal pair of Adam and Eve must have sinned on Tishah B'Av. The Hebrew word for "where are you?" (*ayekah*) is spelled *eichah,* the first word of the Book of Lamentations, which is read on Tishah B'Av.

Shivah

Shivah is the seven-day mourning period following interment during which time many activities are limited. Working or the conducting of business is prohibited. The comfort of wearing leather shoes is denied. A mourner may not bathe or shower for pleasure, use cosmetics, or get a haircut (or shave). Freshly laundered or new clothes are not to be worn. Conjugal relations are prohibited for mourners. And the study of Torah, a sheer delight according to tradition, also is forbidden during shivah.

Laws of Nidah

Nidah literally means "she who is separated." *Nidah* is a state of ritual impurity of a woman as a result of the discharge of blood, usually from the menstrual period. During this period of time, according to Jewish tradition, women are prohibited from sexual relations.

Exile

The traditional notion of exile is that God punished the Jewish people, destroyed the Temple, and dispersed them throughout the world as punishment for not fulfilling their part of the covenant. Referred to as *galut* (or *galus*), it represents not only a physical state but also a state of mind reflecting the historic feeling of the Jewish people for not being able to return to the Land of Israel.

"Cutting k'riah"

The act of tearing the garment of a mourner either at graveside or at the beginning of the funeral service, depending on the custom of the congregation, is referred to as "cutting *k'riah*." In some communities, ribbons are attached to the garment and cut instead of clothing.

The Davidic Kingdom and Its Restoration

David was the second king of Israel (ca. 1000–960 B.C.E.). Under David's reign the tribes of Israel were united and became a nation. One of David's crowning achievements was the capture of Jerusalem from the Jebusites. There he built a new Tabernacle to which he brought the Ark of the Covenant. Jerusalem came to be called the City of David, the heart of his kingdom and the capital of Israel. According to Jewish theology, the Messiah will be a descendant of the line of David, and thus his rule will be established once again and the Temple rebuilt. Reform Judaism has challenged this traditional notion and conceives of a messianic era ushered in by a generation, rather than by one individual.

K'tiv and K'rei

K'tiv is a technical term referring to the way the text is written, and *k'rei* refers to the way it is suggested to be read. This distinction was a compromise suggested by the

Masoretes, the scholar-copyists who added vowels and punctuation to the text in order to maintain a common reading of the text and preserve it. They wanted it to be possible to read and interpret the text correctly without changing the text itself.

GLEANINGS

The Risk of Faith

Faith means risking. Faith means trust in God and ourselves. Ultimately faith is something we do in spite of the consequence.

If we have an ideal or a value and if we are willing to keep faith with it, we will eventually achieve something fine, glowing and wondrous. It could be in a career or in a business. It could be in a cause for others. But the important thing to realize is that our achievement will be tested by the depth of our faith. The challenge comes not in the beginning when it is easy but in the middle when it is tedious and difficult. But those who believe in themselves and their values will find that the risk was worthwhile.

Bernard S. Raskas, *Jewish Spirituality and Faith* (Hoboken, N.J.: KTAV Publishing House, 1989), 16

Working Out

Most people go for annual physical exams as well as to the gym to stay in peak physical condition. Likewise, when it comes to maintaining our psyches, we have self-help books, support groups, and trained professionals there to guide us. To keep our minds sharp, we have courses, books, magazines, and all manner of educational programming. But when it comes to our spirits, our souls, somehow we expect them to be healthy all by themselves.

Every religious tradition provides for daily contact with God. In Judaism, this has meant three worship services (morning, afternoon, and evening). An alternative tradition notes that we ought to find opportunities to say a hundred blessings every day, which includes those said during formal worship. If God is the energy source of the universe, then it is as if we need to plug in our batteries to be recharged each day. Or, understanding God as intimate friend or lover, we want to check in with one another on a regular basis. For some, this will mean attending a regular minyan—the quorum of ten adult Jews required for communal worship—each day. For others, an annual pilgrimage to the synagogue will meet their need. But many of us would like an opportunity for a daily, meaningful connection that fits into the reality of our very busy lives.

Terry Bookman, *The Busy Soul: Ten-Minute Spiritual Workouts Drawn from Jewish Tradition* (New York: Perigee Books, 1999), 14

Between Moments of Pain and Faith

The journey through life is never smooth. It is fraught not only with the day-to-day problems of making ends meet, confronting the challenges associated with our professions, and working at our relationships with those whom we love, but also with the pain of illness, tragedy, separation, and loneliness. These experiences frequently dominate our lives; they can set the tone for the whole journey.

As it is with all of us, my life journey has been like the trek through the desert which the Israelites experienced. There have been times of heightened joy and exaltation, moments of poetry and beauty, but they do not come every day. The test in truth is how to survive and make the best of all those prosaic moments in between.

Norman J. Cohen, "*Etz Chaim Hi:* It Is a Tree of Life," in *Jewish Spiritual Journeys: 20 Essays to Honor the Occasion of the 70th Birthday of Eugene B. Borowitz,* eds. Lawrence A. Hoffman and Arnold Jacob Wolf (West Orange, N.J.: Behrman House, 1997), 74

The Revealing God

God is a revealing God who shows us the way to redemption even in the Holocaust, but his revelation is not clear-cut. It must be discovered by our tapping the heart and soul of God through intuitive insight; by discovering His ways with humankind through historical experience; and by drawing on the mind of God through the spirit of free critical inquiry the power to shape a human destiny worthy of children created in God's image.

God also is a concealing God; for it may be that we shall never know why, with all the power in the world, God should have made himself and his universe so dependent on fragile, tempest-tossed, finite human beings who are as free to break a world as to make one.

Ellis Rivkin, "The Revealing and Concealing God of Israel and Humankind," in *The Life of Covenant: The Challenge of Contemporary Judaism, Essays in Honor of Herman E. Schaalman,* ed. Joseph A. Edelheit (Chicago: Spertus College of Judaica Press, 1986), 171

CHAPTER FOUR

וְשַׁבְתִּי אֲנִי וָאֶרְאֶה אֶת־כָּל־הָעֲשֻׁקִים אֲשֶׁר נַעֲשִׂים תַּחַת הַשָּׁמֶשׁ **ד:א**
וְהִנֵּה דִּמְעַת הָעֲשֻׁקִים וְאֵין לָהֶם מְנַחֵם וּמִיַּד עֹשְׁקֵיהֶם כֹּחַ וְאֵין
לָהֶם מְנַחֵם:

4:1 ONCE AGAIN, I TOOK A LOOK AT ALL THE ACTS OF
OPPRESSION DONE BENEATH THE SUN. BEHOLD:
THE TEARS OF THE OPPRESSED WITH NO ONE TO
COMFORT THEM, AND POWER IN THE HAND OF THEIR
OPPRESSORS WITH NO ONE TO AVENGE THEM.

On the basis of Isaiah 1:24, we have emended the second *m'nacheim* (comforter)
to *m'nakeim* (avenger). Repeating "comforter" seems to make little sense. Ibn Ezra,
on the other hand, accepts the text and both instances of "comforter." He explains
that since they lack power, all the oppressed can do is weep. Even so, such tears
provide no comfort.

וְשַׁבֵּחַ אֲנִי אֶת־הַמֵּתִים שֶׁכְּבָר מֵתוּ מִן־הַחַיִּים אֲשֶׁר הֵמָּה חַיִּים **ד:ב**
עֲדֶנָה:

4:2 THEN I PRAISED THOSE WHO WERE ALREADY DEAD
[FOR THEY] ARE BETTER OFF THAN THOSE WHO ARE
STILL ALIVE.

This is a depressing verse: life is so bad that it is better to be dead than alive. Kohelet
maintains that there is no joy in living for most of humankind. For the *Targum*, being
dead is preferable to being alive, because the dead will be spared the divine
punishment that will be meted out to those still alive. For Rashi, the dead, like the
Patriarchs, over whom the evil inclination *(yetzer hara)* has no influence, are to be
preferred over those who are alive. For Ibn Ezra, it is those for whom death has
brought release from the pain of oppression who are to be preferred over those
alive and still in pain.

ד:ג וְטוֹב מִשְּׁנֵיהֶם אֵת אֲשֶׁר־עֲדֶן לֹא הָיָה אֲשֶׁר לֹא־רָאָה אֶת־
הַמַּעֲשֶׂה הָרָע אֲשֶׁר נַעֲשָׂה תַּחַת הַשָּׁמֶשׁ:

4:3 BETTER THAN BOTH IS TO BE THAT ONE WHO HAS
NEVER YET BEEN, WHO HAS NEVER YET SEEN THE EVIL
DONE BENEATH THE SUN.

Evil does exist, though Kohelet has provided the reader with only a few examples of it. His main complaint has been that he cannot take his wealth with him and must leave it all to strangers when he dies. A person who has amassed the wealth that he has, with the attendant pleasures that such wealth can purchase, can hardly be taken seriously when he bemoans the evil in the world, particularly when he has done little to combat it. However, if he is reflecting on his life from the perspective of old age, perhaps it is his own shortcomings that he regrets.

ד:ד וְרָאִיתִי אֲנִי אֶת־כָּל־עָמָל וְאֵת כָּל־כִּשְׁרוֹן הַמַּעֲשֶׂה כִּי הִיא
קִנְאַת־אִישׁ מֵרֵעֵהוּ גַּם־זֶה הֶבֶל וּרְעוּת רוּחַ:

4:4 I HAVE SEEN ALL THE STRAIN AND SKILL OF HUMAN
ACTIVITY, AND IT IS BUT THE RIVALRY OF ONE PERSON
WITH ANOTHER. THIS TOO IS USELESS AND CHASING
AFTER WIND.

Since wealth, the result of such rivalry, does not descend with us into the grave, all the struggle to attain wealth is ultimately useless. Kohelet claims that even if you win, you still lose in the end. Rivalry is competition. According to Ibn Ezra, all rivalry is based on the desire to have more or better than another.

ד:ה הַכְּסִיל חֹבֵק אֶת־יָדָיו וְאֹכֵל אֶת־בְּשָׂרוֹ:

4:5 THE FOOL FOLDS HIS HANDS AND CONSUMES HIS OWN
FLESH.

The sense of this verse seems to contradict the intent of the previous verse. Perhaps Kohelet is quoting a proverb or folk-saying so that he can refute it. Or, having made a comment that incessant activity is ultimately useless, from the perspective of age Kohelet realizes that the contrary is equally true: indolence has its price. It is as if Kohelet is saying, "Look, the 'rat race' will not get you anywhere, and neither will sitting on your hands. Both are useless." Rashi explains the phrase "consumes one's flesh" as an idiom for shame. The lazy person who steals rather than working will suffer that shame when he or she is eventually judged and condemned as a sinner.

ד:ו טוֹב מְלֹא כַף נָחַת מִמְּלֹא חָפְנַיִם עָמָל וּרְעוּת רוּחַ:

4:6 BETTER A HANDFUL GAINED WITH EASE THAN TWO
HANDFULS GAINED BY STRAIN AND THE CHASING
AFTER WIND.

It is difficult to place this verse. It seems to answer the question posed by the previous
verse and attempt to mediate between it and the verse prior. Effort counts, but not too
much. Rashi takes this verse to suggest a model of behavior: a person should rather be
content with little and thus please the Creator than to strain and displease God.
Ibn Ezra, on the other hand, takes this verse as a model of bad behavior. He feels that
it is the statement of the lazy person who, unwilling to work, is content with little.

ד:ז וְשַׁבְתִּי אֲנִי וָאֶרְאֶה הֶבֶל תַּחַת הַשָּׁמֶשׁ:

4:7 I LOOKED AGAIN AT ANOTHER USELESS THING
BENEATH THE SUN.

Ibn Ezra suggests that Kohelet now turns to another kind of folly, having considered
the lazy fool.

ד:ח יֵשׁ אֶחָד וְאֵין שֵׁנִי גַּם בֵּן וָאָח אֵין־לוֹ וְאֵין קֵץ לְכָל־עֲמָלוֹ גַּם־עֵינָיו
עֵינוֹ לֹא־תִשְׂבַּע עֹשֶׁר.

4:8 HERE IS A PERSON ALL ALONE, WITH NO OFFSPRING
AND NO SIBLING, AND YET THERE IS NO END TO
THE STRAIN AND NO AMOUNT OF WEALTH SATISFIES
THE EYE.

Kohelet can understand that some work to support a family, while some work to
compete against others in society. Nevertheless, he cannot understand a person who
works without a family. Kohelet thinks that such a person asks the question posed by
the next half of the verse.

וּלְמִי אֲנִי עָמֵל וּמְחַסֵּר אֶת־נַפְשִׁי מִטּוֹבָה גַּם־זֶה הֶבֶל וְעִנְיַן
רָע הוּא:

FOR WHOM DO I LABOR AND DEPRIVE MYSELF OF
EVERY PLEASURE? THIS TOO IS USELESS AND A BAD
BUSINESS.

In this second half of the verse, Kohelet presents the model of the person seen too
often in our world, a person who works compulsively, without a purpose and without
a goal. Rashi says that "for whom do I labor?" suggests that this person lacks both a
family and students. Thus, it is not only children that this person lacks, but the person

36

has no disciples on whom to impart wisdom either. The only thing that such a person has is money, which he can't take with him. Our translation of *tovah* as "pleasure" follows Ibn Ezra.

ד:ט טוֹבִים הַשְּׁנַיִם מִן־הָאֶחָד אֲשֶׁר יֵשׁ־לָהֶם שָׂכָר טוֹב בַּעֲמָלָם:

4:9 TWO ARE BETTER THAN ONE, FOR THEY SHALL HAVE
A GOOD REWARD FOR THEIR TOIL.

The three previous verses suggested the folly of a solitary life. Labor has no lasting purpose for the individual bereft of family and friends. This verse and the three verses that follow suggest that being alone is foolish even in the workplace. Working with others is better than working alone because more can be done. Furthermore, the rewards are those of the *joint* enterprise, not the reward itself. Rashi notes that the phrase "two are better than one" applies beyond simply the workplace. One should find a life companion and get married. Ibn Ezra applies the verse to the solitary fool who should find a coworker.

ד:י כִּי אִם־יִפֹּלוּ הָאֶחָד יָקִים אֶת־חֲבֵרוֹ וְאִילוֹ הָאֶחָד שֶׁיִּפּוֹל וְאֵין
שֵׁנִי לַהֲקִימוֹ:

4:10 IF ONE FALLS, THE OTHER CAN HELP HIM [OR HER] GET
UP. IF HE [OR SHE] HAD BEEN ALONE WHEN FALLING,
THE OTHER WOULD NOT BE ABLE TO HELP HIM [OR
HER] GET UP.

The verse begins in a seemingly straightforward manner: a person in business for oneself has no one else to rely on. However, *eilu,* in the second clause, presents a difficulty in this verse. The *Targum* takes the verse to refer to prayer as a means of healing. Thus, for the *Targum, eilu* means "if." Rashi and Ibn Ezra take the word to mean *v'oy lo* (woe to him). Ibn Ezra notes that such usage occurs only in the Book of Kohelet. Critical translations offer both possible translations.

ד:יא גַּם אִם־יִשְׁכְּבוּ שְׁנַיִם וְחַם לָהֶם וּלְאֶחָד אֵיךְ יֵחָם:

4:11 IF TWO LIE TOGETHER, THEY SHALL BE WARM, BUT
HOW CAN ONE ALONE BE WARM?

Continuing the message from the previous verse, Kohelet tells us that sleeping alone is not good either. Rashi understands the verse as a euphemism for sexual intercourse, while Ibn Ezra takes the verse literally.

ד:יב וְאִם־יִתְקְפוֹ הָאֶחָד הַשְּׁנַיִם יַעַמְדוּ נֶגְדּוֹ וְהַחוּט הַמְשֻׁלָּשׁ לֹא בִמְהֵרָה יִנָּתֵק:

4:12 IF ONE WERE TO ATTACK THE TWO, THEY COULD RESIST THE ATTACKER. A THREE-BRAIDED CORD IS NOT EASILY SNAPPED.

A third person as a companion/partner is even better. The virtue is in sharing the effort. The *Targum* understands the verse to refer to those wicked people who incur divine punishment for themselves and others in their generation. The merit of two righteous people would remove that punishment. The merit of three righteous people would even be more efficacious. Rashi gives three interpretations of the verse. It may refer to the attack of robbers. Then again, it may refer to a scholar whose child and grandchild are scholars—since Torah would persist in such a family. Or it may refer to the study of Bible, Mishnah, and proper behavior.

ד:יג טוֹב יֶלֶד מִסְכֵּן וְחָכָם מִמֶּלֶךְ זָקֵן וּכְסִיל אֲשֶׁר לֹא־יָדַע לְהִזָּהֵר עוֹד:

4:13 BETTER A POOR CHILD WHO IS WISE THAN AN OLD KING WHO IS A FOOL, WHO CAN'T EVEN WATCH OUT FOR HIMSELF ANYMORE.

Now Kohelet is no longer interested in companionship, since he has established it as a good thing. Here he reviews a new subject. Better a poor person who understands life than an old king so foolish that he has lost his sense of perspective. A young person still poor is better off than an older person who is rich. Things may yet go well for the young person. Perhaps Kohelet was referring to Joseph, the only biblical character who started off as a prisoner and ended up as a king. The *Targum* applies the verse to Abraham, the "poor child," and to Nimrod as "the old king" (see Levy, *A Faithful Heart*). It preserves the midrash that Abraham knew God at the age of three and thus was "wise," in addition to the midrash that Nimrod, the "fool," cast Abraham into a fiery furnace, from which he was miraculously delivered. Rashi applies the verse to the battle between the *yetzer tov* (good inclination)—the "poor child"—and the *yetzer hara* (evil inclination)—the "old king." For Rashi the last clause refers to the difficulty a foolish older person has in learning.

ד:יד כִּי־מִבֵּית הַסוּרִים יָצָא לִמְלֹךְ כִּי גַּם בְּמַלְכוּתוֹ נוֹלַד רָשׁ:

4:14 FOR ONE CAME OUT OF A PRISON TO RULE EVEN THOUGH HE WAS BORN POOR IN THE KINGDOM.

The last two Hebrew words in the verse, *nolad rash,* present difficulties in interpretation and translation. *Nolad* means "to be born." Some understand the word to mean "to become." *Rash* may mean "poor" (as a noun) or "become poor" (as a verb). Thus, we are presented with three options for the two words *nolad rash*: to be born poor; to become poor; to be born and to become poor. If it is the first option, then the words refer to the "poor child" who was "born poor" in the kingdom and then was elevated to royal status. If we take the second option, the words refer to the "foolish king" who was "to become poor." The third option bridges the two referents: the "poor child" was *nolad* (born) in his kingdom, and it was the "foolish king" who was *rash*, "became poor." Then we are presented with the challenge of translating the last clause as "although he was born poor in his kingdom" or "even during his reign he became poor." There is also the challenge of translating the last clause: "even though one was born poor in the kingdom" (or "even though he was born poor in his kingdom" or "though born a king, he became poor" or "even during his reign he became poor"). To whom does "his reign" refer: the wise child or the foolish king? The *Targum* applies the verse to Abraham and Nimrod. It notes that in the days of Abraham's rule, *itavid Nimrod miskeina* (Nimrod became poor). Rashi understands *nolad* as "became" and, in an application to Joseph and David, interprets the clause to mean that although the poor child (whoever that child might be) was a proper king, he humbled himself before the wise and acted as if he were poor. Basing his interpretation on Job 1:21, Ibn Ezra suggests that the verse "Naked came I from my mother's womb" notes that even a king was born poor. Our translation reflects the simplest understanding of the text.

ד:טו רָאִיתִי אֶת־כָּל־הַחַיִּים הַמְהַלְּכִים תַּחַת הַשֶּׁמֶשׁ עִם הַיֶּלֶד הַשֵּׁנִי אֲשֶׁר יַעֲמֹד תַּחְתָּיו:

4:15 I HAVE LOOKED AT ALL THOSE WHO ARE ALIVE, WHO WALK ABOUT BENEATH THE SUN—WHEN A YOUNG SECOND IN COMMAND RISES IN HIS PLACE.

Kohelet sees people, at any given moment, juxtaposed to a second party, their successors. For example, a young person walks with his or her boss/teacher, whom he or she will later succeed. Kohelet takes a look at both generations. There is no termination for the people. Kohelet sees continuity in succession. Even the young successor will be succeeded—that person, too, will eventually die. But who is this "second in command"? Most take *hasheini* (the second) as the successor, but some scholars suggest that the meaning is disputed. The *Targum* refers to the clash between Rehoboam and Jeroboam ben Nevat and takes *hasheini* to refer to the latter and translates it as "the second." Rashi suggests that the verse is related to the generation of the Flood and maintains that *hayeled hasheini* is the generation that will arise after that generation. Hence, it is difficult to determine whether Rashi understood the term as "second" or "successor." Certainly the *Targum* and possibly Rashi understand the term to indicate yet another "young person" who takes over from the first, as if to say that even the position of the wise young person was not secure. Like so many dynastic struggles, the young person who successfully removed the entrenched older ruler was, in turn, removed by yet another younger person. Ibn Ezra clearly understands *hasheini* as ''successor''—the ''one who reigned after the king.''

ד:טז אֵין־קֵץ לְכָל־הָעָם לְכֹל אֲשֶׁר־הָיָה לִפְנֵיהֶם גַּם הָאַחֲרוֹנִים לֹא יִשְׂמְחוּ־בוֹ כִּי־גַם־זֶה הֶבֶל וְרַעְיוֹן רוּחַ:

4:16 THOSE WHO CAME BEFORE THEM ARE WITHOUT NUMBER. YET THOSE WHO CAME AFTER HIM WILL NOT REJOICE. THIS TOO IS USELESS AND CHASING AFTER WIND.

Ibn Ezra explains that however wise the successor may be, the nature and severity of royal enactments will ensure that succeeding generations find no pleasure in him. Ibn Ezra may reflect the reality of royalty: to live as rulers requires the extraction of considerable wealth from those who are ruled.

ד:יז שְׁמֹר רגליך רַגְלְךָ כַּאֲשֶׁר תֵּלֵךְ אֶל־בֵּית הָאֱלֹהִים וְקָרוֹב לִשְׁמֹעַ מִתֵּת הַכְּסִילִים זָבַח כִּי־אֵינָם יוֹדְעִים לַעֲשׂוֹת רָע:

4:17 WATCH YOUR STEP WHEN YOU GO TO THE HOUSE OF GOD. UNDERSTANDING IS BETTER THAN GIVING SACRIFICES AS FOOLS DO, FOR THEY DON'T EVEN KNOW HOW TO DO EVIL.

The end of the verse is problematic: what is it that fools do or don't do? The *Targum* explains that though fools bring sacrifices, they don't repent and hence can't gain God's favor. Thus, they don't know how to do good or evil. Rashi explains that fools do not realize when they do harm to themselves. Ibn Ezra proposes three possible interpretations of what fools do or don't do. First, he suggests dividing the Hebrew of the clause into two parts: *ki einam yodim, laasot ra,* ''not knowing, they do evil.'' Second, he proposes that since fools don't know how to do evil, how much less do they know how to do good. And finally, Ibn Ezra vocalizes *ra* as *reia* to mean ''favor'' (possibly on the basis of Psalm 139:2); thus, fools don't know how to act to gain favor. Our translation follows Ibn Ezra's second suggestion, which accepts Kohelet's contempt for fools. Fools know nothing—neither what religion means in order to gain divine favor, nor even how to sin in order to incur divine disfavor.

Nimrod

Nimrod was a descendant of Cush, the son of Ham, the first who claimed to be a ''mighty one in the earth.'' Nimrod's kingdom began with Babel, which he gradually enlarged (Genesis 10:8–10). The ''land of Nimrod'' (Micah 5:5) is a designation of Assyria or of Shinar, which is a part of it.

Good Inclination and Evil Inclination

The Rabbis identified two complementary sets of drives that coexist in each person. One set of drives, which may be classified as libidinal drives or urges and include sex, hunger, and the like, are grouped under the term *yetzer hara* (the inclination to evil). While these drives are not evil in themselves, left unchecked, they may lead the individual to evil. For example, while the sexual drive may lead the individual to procreate, it can also lead to lust and illicit sexual behavior. The hunger drive will lead the individual to nourish the body with food, but it can also lead to obesity. The *yetzer hara* is kept in balance by the *yetzer hatov* (the inclination to do good). Similarly, these drives must be kept in balance by the *yetzer hara*. According to this understanding, individuals who may want to give *tzedakah,* for example, run the risk of placing themselves or their family in jeopardy should they give all their money to charitable causes.

Rehoboam

The name Rehoboam literally means "he enlarges the people." At forty-one, Rehoboam succeeded Solomon on the throne. He was apparently his only son. His mother was Naamah, a well-known Ammonite princess. Rehoboam reigned for seventeen years, from 975 to 958 B.C.E. Although he was acknowledged at once as the rightful heir to the throne, the people expressed a desire to modify the character of the theocratic government. They felt that the taxation levied during Solomon's reign was particularly burdensome and oppressive. Thus, the people assembled at Shechem and demanded a reduction in their taxes. Rehoboam met them at Shechem and listened to their demands for relief. After three days, having consulted with a younger generation of advisors who had grown up around him, he answered the people haughtily instead of following the advice of elders. This brought matters speedily to a crisis. As a result, the kingdom was divided. Rehoboam was appalled and tried to make concessions to appease the people, but it was too late. The kingdom of Judah decayed rapidly. Rehoboam died at age fifty-eight and was succeeded by his son Abijah (I Kings 12, II Chronicles 10).

Jeroboam ben Nevat

The name Jeroboam literally means "increase of the people." He was the son of Nevat, the first king of the ten tribes, over whom he reigned for twenty-two years (976–945 B.C.E.). He was the son of a widow of Zeredah. While still young, he was promoted by Solomon to be chief superintendent of bands of forced laborers. Influenced by the words of the prophet Ahijah, he began to form conspiracies with the view of becoming king of the ten tribes. When his intentions were discovered, he fled to Egypt, where he remained for a length of time under the protection of Shishak I (I Kings 11:26–40). On the death of Solomon, the ten tribes, having revolted, invited

Jeroboam to become their king. The conduct of Rehoboam favored the designs of Jeroboam, and Jeroboam was accordingly proclaimed "king of Israel" (I Kings 12:1–20). He rebuilt and fortified Shechem as the capital of his kingdom. He perpetuated the division thus made between the two parts of the kingdom by erecting "golden calves" at Dan and Bethel, the two ends of his kingdom. He told the people to refrain from making pilgrimage to Jerusalem and instead to bring their offerings to the shrines he had erected (I Kings 12:25–30). Thus he became distinguished as the man who caused Israel to sin. This policy was followed by all the succeeding kings of Israel.

Jeroboam discontinued his worship at shrines as a result of the intervention of a prophet of Judah who appeared before him while he was engaged in offering incense at Bethel. Instead of listening to the prophet's warning, Jeroboam tried to arrest him. But his strength was "dried up," and the altar before which he stood was torn apart. Only after his desperate plea "was his hand restored him again" (I Kings 13:1–6). Nevertheless, the miracle of healing made no abiding impression on him and he continued to war with the House of Judah. He died soon after his son Abijah.

Generation of the Flood

The generation of the Flood are those who lived in Noah's generation, during the time of the flood that destroyed nearly all of humanity. The Torah states of this generation, "The earth was corrupted before God and filled with violence" (Genesis 6:11). Rashi explains that corruption in this case means sexual immorality and idolatry and that violence means robbery. These activities provoked God to destroy civilization. Some verses earlier, we are told that "the sons of God saw the daughters of man that they were fair, and they took for themselves wives, whomsoever they chose" (Genesis 6:2). Apparently, this generation of males was promiscuous and sought all types of sexual gratification without any moral restrictions. So God gave the people their first warning and offered 120 years to change their behavior. But the text tells us that the behavior continued: "God saw that the wickedness of humans was great on the earth, and that every imagination of the thoughts of the heart was only evil continually" (Genesis 6:5).

GLEANINGS

The Search for God

We tend to think of our search as a solitary one, between an individual and God. Judaism suggests that the quest is shared. This is the meaning of covenant, a communal contract between us and God that each person fulfills. We learn this from the commandment for circumcision. God says: All that ignore this shall be cut off from their kin. Not from God, but from the community.

Perhaps the extensive comfort and security possessed by American Jewry frees us to hear God's voice differently from the way a persecuted community might. Indeed, freedom is our reality. The current trend toward spiritual life reflects a desire for more than personal fulfillment. We want to be part of something greater than our individual selves. We yearn for true community. We seek God. And God's voice need not be heard as stern and commanding. God is the blessed Holy One: loving, caring, and seeking relationship with us.

Elyse D. Frishman, "A Voice in the Dark: How Do We Hear God?" in *Duties of the Soul: The Role of Commandments in Liberal Judaism*, eds. Niles E. Goldstein and Peter S. Knobel (New York: UAHC Press, 1999), 125

Work Can Be Slavery

On the gates of Auschwitz were written the infamous words *"Arbeit macht frei,"* "Work shall set you free." This was the grim lie of the Nazi work camps [an obscene allusion to the liberating formula of the Middle Ages *Stadtluft macht frei,* "The air of the city makes one free," that is, a serf who gets to a city gained new status as a free person]: Work would bring freedom to the worker. But Auschwitz was the antithesis of freedom. Its purpose was to confirm slavery and extract a death of the body and spirit from the worker.

In a sense, a small hidden spark of the mentality of Auschwitz lingers in our world. These are the fruits of that mentality: If we judge ourselves and judge others only by the goods or services that we produce, if we believe that to *be* more is to *do* more, then we are truly slaves to what we do. Work becomes an end in itself.

We eventually conclude that if we are *only* what we do, then to be "more," we must do more and produce more. This is no less than the demonic lie of Auschwitz. Instead of liberating us, work enslaves and owns us.

Jeffrey K. Salkin, *Being God's Partner: How to Find the Hidden Link Between Spirituality and Your Work* (Woodstock, Vt.: Jewish Lights Publishing, 1994), 147

God's Uniqueness

The story opens with the depiction of an idolatrous, immoral world ruled by King Nimrod, originally mentioned in Genesis 10:9 as a "mighty hunter." Nimrod exalts himself as a god. The people of his era serve and worship him.

Nimrod, a skilled astrologer, predicts that a boy will be born who will usurp the king's faith. By means of a royal decree, Nimrod murders seventy thousand infants to prevent this.

When the angels on high witness this rampant slaughter, they ask God whether the Holy One is aware of the evil that has occurred. God replies in the affirmative and assures that not only does God see, but they soon will see how the power of the Divine will be used to administer justice vis-à-vis Nimrod.

Thus, the midrash sets the stage for a contest that pits God's might versus earthly (tyrannical) power. The text presents Abraham's birth as the first chapter in this struggle, as Nimrod's murderous decree places the future Patriarch's very existence in immediate peril.

In this way, Abraham's emergence serves as a metaphor for the birth of all positive turns in life in which the initial hours prove critical. Success is dependent not just on the actions of humans but also on divine help. This is true in terms of both physical and spiritual survival. Whether major surgery is successful often is apparent only after the passing of forty-eight hours. In such a case, the doctors do all they can do, but a positive outcome ultimately depends upon the realm beyond that of human hands.

Benjamin Levy, A Faithful Heart: Preparing for the High Holy Days
(New York: UAHC Press, 2001), 3

"Know Before Whom You Stand"

Who is your boss? To whom do you answer? Who has the power? Who makes the final decisions? Who holds the ultimate authority?

Is it your customer, who orders from you? Is it your supervisor, who gives you your assignments? Is it the owner, who signs your checks? Is it the board of directors, who must ratify your decisions? Is it the stockholders, who must approve your plan? Is it yourself, on whom all responsibility falls?

No matter who it may be, no matter what person seems to control your fate and your destiny, there is something else that is your real boss, something else that fashions your work and molds your conduct.

There is something beyond you, something greater than you, that defines and shapes you, that sets out for you standards of right and wrong, that demands your goodness and calls you to greatness.

Some people call it intuition. Some call it gut feeling. Some call it conscience. Some call it the inner force. Some call it the higher spirit.

Some call it God.

No mater what you call it, it is always present, summoning you to heed its commands.

And you are always in its presence, compelling you to know before whom you stand.

Wayne Dosick, The Business Bible: Ten Commandments for Creating an Ethical Workplace
(New York: William Morrow and Company, 1993), 179–80

CHAPTER FIVE

ה:א אַל־תְּבַהֵל עַל־פִּיךָ וְלִבְּךָ אַל־יְמַהֵר לְהוֹצִיא דָבָר לִפְנֵי הָאֱלֹהִים
כִּי הָאֱלֹהִים בַּשָּׁמַיִם וְאַתָּה עַל־הָאָרֶץ עַל־כֵּן יִהְיוּ דְבָרֶיךָ
מְעַטִּים:

**5:1 DON'T LET YOUR MIND DRIVE YOU NOR YOUR MOUTH
RUSH YOU TO SPEAK BEFORE GOD. SINCE GOD IS IN
HEAVEN AND YOU ARE ON EARTH, YOUR WORDS
SHOULD BE FEW.**

Lifnei haElohim refers to the point of view of the person addressing God. In other
words, be careful. No matter where you are, realize that God hears everything.
Watch your words in the Temple, and at all other times as well. *Lev* (mind) refers to
intent, while *pi* (mouth) is the ability to express it. Do not rush to speak just to get
"something off your chest." In this verse Ibn Ezra finds justification for his opposition
to the insertion of the *piyutim* (liturgical poetry), particularly those of Eliezer Kalir,
into the liturgy.

ה:ב כִּי בָּא הַחֲלוֹם בְּרֹב עִנְיָן וְקוֹל כְּסִיל בְּרֹב דְּבָרִים:

**5:2 JUST AS A DREAM CONTAINS MANY MATTERS, SO DOES
A FOOL'S SPEECH CONTAIN MANY WORDS.**

Chalom (dream) and *inyan* (matter) are contrasted in this verse. While there will be
many who disagree, including modern psychoanalysts, Kohelet suggests that just as
dreams are filled with things that are meaningless, similarly lacking in meaning are the
many words of a fool. A familiar notion is being repeated: the fool speaks, but the
wise person thinks.

ה:ג כַּאֲשֶׁר תִּדֹּר נֶדֶר לֵאלֹהִים אַל־תְּאַחֵר לְשַׁלְּמוֹ כִּי אֵין חֵפֶץ
בַּכְּסִילִים אֵת אֲשֶׁר־תִּדֹּר שַׁלֵּם:

**5:3 WHEN YOU MAKE A VOW TO GOD, DON'T DELAY
PAYING IT. GOD TAKES NO PLEASURE IN FOOLS.
WHATEVER YOU VOW, PAY.**

One may look at this verse and think that it is a contradiction of the final verse of
the previous chapter (4:17) and the first verse of this chapter (5:1). If we have

45

distinguished between the wise person who understands and the fool who merely brings sacrifices, and between the wise person who speaks little and the fool who speaks much, one might be inclined to question why a wise person would have to be warned about paying vows. Yet, it is the fool who would make a vow and then pay his or her vows most promptly. The image of God so far presented in Kohelet is that of a Deity far removed from the concerns of humankind. Such a God would be the God conceived of by a wise person. By contrast, the God worshiped by the "fool" would be the God who is intimately concerned with humankind and the day-to-day challenges of the individual and everyday living. Thus, the fool would make vows and be most concerned about paying those vows. Maybe Kohelet is teaching theology. Perhaps he is quoting a familiar proverb in order to deceive the unsuspecting reader into thinking that the author is more pious than he really is. Or perhaps Kohelet has changed his perspective on life and living, and we, like him, have found a way to balance both perspectives on God.

ה:ד טוֹב אֲשֶׁר לֹא־תִדֹּר מִשֶּׁתִּדּוֹר וְלֹא תְשַׁלֵּם:

5:4 BETTER NOT TO VOW [AT ALL] THAN TO MAKE A VOW
   AND NOT PAY.

Perhaps Kohelet is advising us that it is best not to make vows at all. In speaking without thinking, individuals do not realize or recognize the implications of their own words. Fools are those who do not care about the implications of their words or of their vows.

ה:ה אַל־תִּתֵּן אֶת־פִּיךָ לַחֲטִיא אֶת־בְּשָׂרֶךָ וְאַל־תֹּאמַר לִפְנֵי הַמַּלְאָךְ
   כִּי שְׁגָגָה הִיא לָמָּה יִקְצֹף הָאֱלֹהִים עַל־קוֹלֶךָ וְחִבֵּל אֶת־מַעֲשֵׂה
   יָדֶיךָ:

5:5 DON'T LET YOUR MOUTH MAKE YOUR BODY SUFFER,
   CAUSING YOU TO HAVE TO SAY BEFORE AN ANGEL
   THAT IT WAS A MISTAKE. WHY SHOULD GOD GET
   ANGRY AT YOUR VOICE AND DESTROY WHAT YOU
   HAVE ACCOMPLISHED?

This problematic verse assumes a rather anthropomorphic/anthropopathic concept of God, a God who is concerned about human beings. While this is indeed the God who is conceived of in biblical and Rabbinic Judaism, it seems to be different from the concept that we have already seen elsewhere in the book. Some will argue that this is contradictory. Others will argue that this idea was added by an editor to soften the other approach. And still others will argue that this is an understanding about God that Kohelet arrived at late in his life. *Lachati* (to cause to sin), as Rashi points out, means to "suffer" the consequences of one's sin. *B'sarecha* (your flesh), as Ibn Ezra points out, means "your body." For the *Targum, hamalach* is the cruel angel *(malacha achzara)*. For Rashi, it is simply "the messenger sent to collect the charity you allotted." For Ibn Ezra, it is the divine angel who is charged to record human statements. "The work of your hands" *(et maaseih yadecha)* is translated literally by the *Targum* as *yat ovadei y'dach,* but as *mitzvot shehayu b'yadecha* (the commandments you possessed) by Rashi. Our translation of "what you have accomplished" is an attempt to bridge the literal meaning with an idiomatic one.

הו כִּי בְרֹב חֲלֹמוֹת וַהֲבָלִים וּדְבָרִים הַרְבֵּה כִּי אֶת־הָאֱלֹהִים יְרָא:

5:6 In spite of many dreams, useless notions, and
words, fear God.

This is a difficult verse, because how the text is read will determine its content. The challenge begins with the first phrase. *V'rov* can mean "with many" or "in spite of many." Reading it as "with many" would suggest that Kohelet is being ironic, even bordering on heresy, for what kind of God would be "feared" with "dreams, useless notions, and words"? Perhaps Kohelet is using intentionally ambiguous language, a technique common in the Middle Ages. Perhaps Kohelet is merely quoting a proverb familiar to his contemporary readers in order to direct his words to a particular group of people in order to conceal the heterodox quality of the book (providing you accept the possibility that it is heterodox, rather than the writing from the perspective of advanced age). Kohelet's use of "fear God" is also puzzling. The *Targum* presents the reader with Rabbinic Judaism's understanding of the term, in which *v'rov* is taken to mean "in many" and translates, "Don't believe in the many dreams of the false prophets, or in the useless notions of the sorcerers, or in the many words of the wicked, but rather serve the wise righteous persons and receive instruction from them; and revere God." Thus, "fearing God" is the service of the righteous and the receiving of instruction. Rashi's comment follows the *Targum.* Although Ibn Ezra holds a view similar to Rashi's, he presents an alternate: all speech is permissible as long as God is mentioned.

הז אִם־עֹשֶׁק רָשׁ וְגֵזֶל מִשְׁפָּט וָצֶדֶק תִּרְאֶה בַמְּדִינָה אַל־תִּתְמַהּ
עַל־הַחֵפֶץ כִּי גָבֹהַּ מֵעַל גָּבֹהַּ שֹׁמֵר וּגְבֹהִים עֲלֵיהֶם:

5:7 If you see the oppression of the poor and
the corruption of justice in a society, don't
be surprised about it, even though there is a
supervisor over them and others over him
[or her].

Ki presents the pivotal difficulty in the verse. It can mean "because," "for," "if," or "even though." It has the last meaning in this verse. Kohelet tells his reader that

Kohelet: A Modern Commentary on Ecclesiastes

corruption in society is not prevented by supervision. Rather, it is abetted by such. Corruption lower down in society is often made possible by paying off people higher up the ladder. Although the *Targum* and Rashi take *shomeir* (guard, supervisor) to mean God, and Ibn Ezra alludes to a specific real-life situation on which he does not elaborate, most moderns take the term to refer to a human guard.

ה:ח וְיִתְרוֹן אֶרֶץ בַּכֹּל הִיא הוּא מֶלֶךְ לְשָׂדֶה נֶעֱבָד:

5:8 THE GREATEST PROFIT IS IN AGRICULTURE; EVEN A SOVEREIGN RULER IS DEPENDENT ON THE FIELD.

Our translation follows Ibn Ezra. He thinks that agriculture is the best way to make a living, because even a sovereign ruler at the top of a society is compelled to turn to the products of the soil in order to live.

ה:ט אֹהֵב כֶּסֶף לֹא־יִשְׂבַּע כֶּסֶף וּמִי־אֹהֵב בֶּהָמוֹן לֹא תְבוּאָה גַּם־זֶה הָבֶל:

5:9 ONE WHO LOVES MONEY WILL NEVER HAVE ENOUGH. ONE WHO LOVES WEALTH WILL NEVER GET ENOUGH. THIS ALSO IS USELESS.

The *Targum* refers the verse to matters of business practice, taking the first clause to apply to the *g'var tagar* (traveling merchant) and the second clause to apply to the *marei pragmatiah* (business person). The first individual can't acquire money, and the second can't amass it. [In the Middle Ages, Jews were prohibited from working in the guilds as craftsmen. Therefore, they became merchants and moneylenders. Keeping in mind their roles, one can understand Rashi taking the "money" to refer to Torah and "wealth" to refer to the rest of the Bible, the Mishnah, and the Gemara.]

ה:י בִּרְבוֹת הַטּוֹבָה רַבּוּ אוֹכְלֶיהָ וּמַה־כִּשְׁרוֹן לִבְעָלֶיהָ כִּי אִם־רְאִית רְאוּת עֵינָיו:

5:10 THE MORE YOU POSSESS, THE MORE THERE IS TO CONSUME, SO WHAT ADVANTAGE IS THERE IN POSSESSING OTHER THAN ENJOYING WHAT YOU SEE?

This comes to nothing also. As might be expected, Rashi takes the verse to refer to Torah and mitzvot, while Ibn Ezra takes the verse to refer literally to material possessions.

ה:יא מְתוּקָה שְׁנַת הָעֹבֵד אִם־מְעַט וְאִם־הַרְבֵּה יֹאכֵל וְהַשָּׂבָע לֶעָשִׁיר
אֵינֶנּוּ מַנִּיחַ לוֹ לִישׁוֹן:

5:11 The laborer's sleep is sweet, whether eating
little or much. The rich person's plenty does
not allow for sleep.

This individual worries about being robbed. Stored-up treasures end up as a
misfortune to their owner. Rashi takes the "laborer" to be an agricultural laborer who
has become accustomed to the scarcity of food. The "rich person" is the wealthy
merchant who is anxious at night about his or her merchandise. Perhaps it is a
reflection of Ibn Ezra's world when he tells the reader that the "rich person" worries
day and night about possessions that might be seized by the king, taken violently, or
stolen by thieves. This verse brings to mind the twentieth-century writer Sholom
Aleichem's biting comment about wealth causing the wealthy to suffer. He joked that
if the rich could hire someone to die for them, at least the poor could then make a
living! Perhaps implicit in the verse is a lament that few wealthy people would be
willing to cast away their wealth so that they might enjoy a simple life, a simple diet,
and the "sweet sleep" of the laborer.

ה:יב יֵשׁ רָעָה חוֹלָה רָאִיתִי תַּחַת הַשָּׁמֶשׁ עֹשֶׁר שָׁמוּר לִבְעָלָיו לְרָעָתוֹ:

5:12 There is a horrendous evil that I have seen
beneath the sun: a fortune is accumulated to
the detriment of its owner.

Such individuals store up wealth before having children. If they then have children,
they have already lost their fortune by that time. If you try to store it up for the future,
the future may not be there. Ibn Ezra attempts to explain *raah cholah* (horrendous
evil) as coming either from the root *chalah* (thus, "sick evil") or from the root *chil*
(thus, "evil that happens"). Rashi applies the verse to Korach, who, according to
Jewish tradition, was extremely wealthy. He also rebelled against Moses' authority and
therefore against God, who appointed Moses. Rashi implies that his accumulation of
wealth was key to his rejection of authority and his own demise. However, the verse
as it stands may present the reader with a problem: in a mercantile community, the
amassing of capital is thought to bring success rather than failure. If it brings failure,
then it is indeed a "horrendous evil" or a "sick evil." How the "evil" happens is
suggested by the verse that follows.

ה:יג וְאָבַד הָעֹשֶׁר הַהוּא בְּעִנְיַן רָע וְהוֹלִיד בֵּן וְאֵין בְּיָדוֹ מְאוּמָה:

5:13 IF THIS FORTUNE IS LOST IN SOME BAD VENTURE, AND
IF HE [OR SHE] THEN BEGETS A CHILD, THERE WILL BE
NOTHING IN HIS [OR HER] HAND.

It was not the accumulation of wealth itself that caused the problem. Rather, it was the losing of it. It would seem that Kohelet is constantly tortured by the fact that an individual's wealth does not transcend the grave. Even were one to have a child and thus have the possibility of passing on the wealth to someone who could be an extension of oneself, it is still not guaranteed that the wealth would not be lost before the child was able to inherit it.

ה:יד כַּאֲשֶׁר יָצָא מִבֶּטֶן אִמּוֹ עָרוֹם יָשׁוּב לָלֶכֶת כְּשֶׁבָּא וּמְאוּמָה לֹא־יִשָּׂא בַעֲמָלוֹ שֶׁיֹּלֵךְ בְּיָדוֹ:

5:14 NAKED FROM YOUR MOTHER'S WOMB YOU CAME, AND
SO WILL YOU RETURN, COMING BACK AS YOU WENT
OUT, BRINGING NOTHING FOR YOUR TOIL THAT YOU
COULD CARRY IN YOUR HAND.

While the original verse is in the masculine third person, we have translated it in the gender-neutral second person. Each individual must go back (*k'sheba*, "to return to the starting point," that is, to death). And none of us can take our wealth to the grave, however meager or grand. Both the *Targum* and Rashi understand being "naked" as being without virtue. Ibn Ezra understands the verse to refer to possessions. It is unclear whether the person intended is the parent mentioned in 5:13 or the child. In any case, this verse again reminds the reader of the lesson that Kohelet has learned: you can't take it with you.

ה:טו וְגַם־זֹה רָעָה חוֹלָה כָּל־עֻמַּת שֶׁבָּא כֵּן יֵלֵךְ וּמַה־יִּתְרוֹן לוֹ שֶׁיַּעֲמֹל לָרוּחַ:

5:15 AND THIS TOO IS A HORRENDOUS EVIL: IN THE SAME
WAY YOU CAME, YOU WILL GO, SO WHAT WAS YOUR
GAIN THAT YOU SHOULD STRAIN FOR THE WIND?

Like the previous verse, we have translated this in the second person. Similarly, it is unclear whether the reference is to the parent or child. In either case, death ends the mortal journey of the human. Our possessions are meaningless when we are dead.

ה:טז גַּם כָּל־יָמָיו בַּחֹשֶׁךְ יֹאכֵל וְכָעַס הַרְבֵּה וְחָלְיוֹ וָקָצֶף:

5:16 ALL YOUR DAYS, YOU EAT IN DARKNESS WITH MUCH
VEXATION, ILLNESS, AND ANGER.

Since this verse continues the theme established several verses ago, we have continued our style of translating in the second person. The individual eats in frustration
and reaps anger, while basically blind to what lies ahead. The *Targum* explains why
this person eats "in darkness" (*d'lachmohi vilchodohi ta'im*, "because he eats his
bread alone"). This is a sad picture of an individual who possesses money but lacks
friends and family. Ibn Ezra thinks that the person described is so bent on making
money that he or she devotes all the daylight hours to business and waits until late at
night to eat. Without a doubt, such a person will suffer "vexation, illness, and anger."

ה:יז הִנֵּה אֲשֶׁר־רָאִיתִי אָנִי טוֹב אֲשֶׁר־יָפֶה לֶאֱכוֹל־וְלִשְׁתּוֹת וְלִרְאוֹת
טוֹבָה בְּכָל־עֲמָלוֹ שֶׁיַּעֲמֹל תַּחַת־הַשֶּׁמֶשׁ מִסְפַּר יְמֵי־חַיָּיו אֲשֶׁר־
נָתַן־לוֹ הָאֱלֹהִים כִּי־הוּא חֶלְקוֹ:

5:17 I NOW HAVE SEEN THAT IT IS GOOD AND RIGHT TO
EAT AND DRINK AND HAVE PLEASURE FROM ALL THE
LABOR THAT ONE HAS EXPENDED BENEATH THE SUN,
ACCORDING TO THE NUMBER OF DAYS OF LIFE THAT
GOD HAS GIVEN. FOR THAT IS THE PORTION THAT
ONE HAS.

Our rendering of *tov asher yafeh* as "it is good and right" follows the *Targum*'s
translation *tava hu livnei enasha ud'shapir l'hon*: "it is good for humans and fine for
them." It seems that Kohelet has now concluded that if death brings an end to
everything and if one lacks family or friends to whom to pass one's wealth, one might
as well enjoy wealth while able to do so. Since such a focus on the enjoyment of this
world might seem troubling to some who maintain a traditionalist view of text, Rashi
takes the verse to refer to the study of Torah.

ה:יח גַּם כָּל־הָאָדָם אֲשֶׁר נָתַן־לוֹ הָאֱלֹהִים עֹשֶׁר וּנְכָסִים וְהִשְׁלִיטוֹ
לֶאֱכֹל מִמֶּנּוּ וְלָשֵׂאת אֶת־חֶלְקוֹ וְלִשְׂמֹחַ בַּעֲמָלוֹ זֹה מַתַּת אֱלֹהִים
הִיא:

5:18 THIS IS A GIFT FROM GOD: TO BE THAT PERSON TO
WHOM GOD HAS GIVEN WEALTH AND POSSESSIONS AND
THE POWER TO CONSUME THEM, TO TAKE ONE'S
PORTION, TO REJOICE IN ONE'S TOIL.

This verse carries forward the sentiment contained in the previous verse: to have
possessions is not enough; one has to have the opportunity to enjoy them as well.

The *Targum* hopes that the person to whom God has given possessions in this life will use them to give charity in order to merit the life to come. Rashi's comments follow the *Targum*.

הֵ:יֹט כִּי לֹא הַרְבֵּה יִזְכֹּר אֶת־יְמֵי חַיָּיו כִּי הָאֱלֹהִים מַעֲנֶה בְּשִׂמְחַת
לִבּוֹ:

5:19 ONE WILL NOT LONG REMEMBER THE DAYS OF ONE'S LIFE, BUT GOD WILL PROVIDE THE JOYS OF LIFE.

Maaneh in the last clause presents a problem of translation and interpretation. On the basis of Job 32:5, Rashi takes *maaneh* (answer) as a noun. Ibn Ezra takes it as a verb, meaning "provide" or "answer." Koehler and Baumgartner (p. 854) take it as a verb: "keep one busy." The last clause then affects the understanding of the first part of the verse. According to Rashi, since the days of this life are few and not worth remembering, one should not labor to gain transitory riches. Rather, one should work for the lasting wealth (that is, Torah): God is the one who provides the joy of life. According to Ibn Ezra's first view, it is important to keep in mind that although the days of one's life may be limited, God provides what little joy there is in them. According to Ibn Ezra's second view, although a person's life may be short, God will provide the answer for the individual's questions of what joy one has. According to Ibn Ezra's second perspective, people do not remember the days of their lives because they are distracted by their enjoyment of them.

Piyutim

A *piyut* (sing.) is a liturgical poem that has been inserted into a fixed prayer. The genre is thought to have emerged in the Land of Israel around the fifth century. They were subsequently composed in other communities, to a limited extent in Babylonia and then in great numbers in Germany, France, Spain, and Italy. The writing of *piyutim* reached its zenith in the fourteenth century, though *piyutim* continued to be composed through the eighteenth century. The *piyutim* from the latter period were rarely added to the fixed liturgy of the synagogue. The emergence of prayer books that were mass produced limited the opportunity for the addition of new creations.

Eliezer Kalir

Kalir (sixth to seventh century) was probably the most famous and influential of the early liturgical poets. While he refers to his hometown as Kiryat Sefer, its precise identification is not clear and may be Sephoris in the Galilee in Israel. His poetry is filled with allusions to the midrash, and his use of Hebrew shows much creativity and innovation. As a result, though, it is often difficult to determine the exact meaning of his words. Ibn Ezra, like others, was critical of Kalir's writings. In his comment on

Kohelet 5:1, Ibn Ezra states his criticism of Kalir's poems: "They are not clear. They are filled with more riddle than meaning. They are written in a jargon of Hebrew mixed with Aramaic. Even the Hebrew makes little sense, since the words are used incorrectly. They are filled with midrashim that distort the quoted Hebrew texts." The traditional Ashkenazic *machzor* contains approximately 200 of his compositions. Many of his writings were discovered in the Cairo Genizah. There are those who said that Kalir helped revive Hebrew as a literary language, that is, a language in which people wrote instead of just being a language that people read.

Korach

Korach, a Levite, was the son of Izhar, son of Kohat, who led a rebellion in the desert against the leadership and authority of Moses and Aaron. Other Levites and Israelites joined him. The Torah relates the story of the rebellion in Numbers 16. According to some scholars, the story seems to be an amalgamation of three separate traditions concerning this rebellion. One tradition focuses on Datan and Abiram, members of the tribe of Reuben, and reflects the bitter feelings of that tribe. They did not like what they perceived as the preferred status of Moses and Aaron and were punished for their actions by being swallowed by the earth. A second tradition is concerned with the 250 Israelites who revolted against the exclusive leadership of Moses. They were consumed by divine fire. And the third tradition included Korach's challenge to the exclusive right of Aaron and his priests to serve God. They argued that all Levites should have the right to do so, not only Aaron and his descendants. Moses did not even entertain the complaint.

It may be that the Korach rebellion reflected the centralization of worship in Jerusalem with the attendant "downsizing" of the priesthood. Since we have evidence (e.g., Judges 17:10) that the Levites served as priests and since we have the phrase *hakohanim hal'viim* (Deuteronomy 17:9), it may be argued that the Korach story is a retrojection seeking to establish one branch of the Levites as *the* priests in *the* sanctuary. The remaining Levites could work nowhere else and could only get jobs as assistants to the priests. Anyone objecting to such downsizing would receive the answer: such was the decree of God. More than that: make any trouble and the earth will open up beneath you and swallow you! The midrash *(Tanchuma, Korach)* makes the Korach story a polemic against rationalism. Korach asked perfectly reasonable questions: If a garment is all *t'chelet* (a spelled blue), then why does it need a fringe of *t'chelet*? If a room is filled with *sifrei Torah* (Torah scrolls), then why does it need a mezuzah? Korach's objection to the centralization of civil power in Moses and religious power in Aaron was also valid. However, if the demands of religion were clear, there would be no need for revelation.

GLEANINGS

The Tao of Judaism

We cannot change the human condition. So, how do we live life, love life, affirm life, bring children into the world, how do we celebrate life, knowing the truth about being human, aware of the fragility of human life? The answer is: *Tshuva, tefila, tzedaka*. This is the way Jewish tradition teaches for getting through life, for overcoming and transcending the anguish of human existence, for transforming the human condition. These are not three separate acts, three distinct moments, but rather three steps along one path—the way of Jewish wisdom. *Tshuva, tefila, tzedaka* are what in Eastern traditions might be called the Tao of Judaism—the pathway of enlightenment. Let us follow the path.

In a moral sense, *tshuva* means to repent. Literally, *tshuva* means to turn. To turn inward. To return. To come home. It also means to answer—how we answer the human condition, the terrifying fragility of life.

Edward Feinstein, "The Tao of Judaism"
(Rosh HaShanah sermon, Valley Beth Shalom, Encino, Calif., 1996), 2–3

The Paradox of Living

Trying to find a theology of healing that makes sense in the post-modern world presents us with a paradox. While science informs much of how we navigate the world today, we have come to understand its shortcomings. Instead, we learn that religion is more helpful in unraveling the mysteries of the world. Among other things, we have learned that the questions we ask are often more important than the answers that science provides. It seems to be part of the human condition to be simultaneously rational and metarational. Thus, our beliefs about God and healing should be constructed along a progressive continuum that reflects the various stages of our suffering and our faith. We experience different facets of God as we move through our lives, and our belief in God changes as we progress through these experiences. Similarly, we confront different aspects of God as healer as we move forward on our path toward healing. Thus, our theology of healing changes as well. Our journey is dynamic. As a result, so is our theology. There are times in which we keenly feel the power of God's healing presence. It may overwhelm us, filling us with awe and dread. At other times, God seems distant and remote. It appears as though God is disinterested in the world and disconnected from our individual human lives. In part, this sense of alienation and estrangement is a dividend of living at this juncture in history, which challenges us with the paradox in the first place.

The philosopher/theologian Martin Buber argued that evil may be defined as the absence of relationship and direction in our lives. Since the model for all of our relationships should reflect the one we establish with God, we can potentially combat the evil of suffering by developing relations with each other and with God.

Such a process will help us recognize that we are never alone: God is always there alongside us wherever we go, whatever we are forced to confront in our lives. This will bring the healing presence of God to our midst, bringing healing to the body through the soul.

Kerry M. Olitzky, *Jewish Paths toward Healing and Wholeness: A Personal Guide to Dealing with Suffering* (Woodstock, Vt.: Jewish Lights Publishing, 2000), 21–22

The Role of the Mentor

Almost every Jew who is involved in communal Jewish living can recall an older relative (or neighbor) who provided precious memories of Jewish holy days, Sabbaths, and festivals. Whether born Jewish or someone who has chosen to be Jewish, we have all been touched by a grandparent, an in-law, or a dear friend and mentor who invited us over for a Pesah Seder, showed us how to bake a hallah, or took the time to explain and share the lighting of Hanukkah candles.

It is no exaggeration that those living experiences are essential to instilling a passion for Judaism and the Jewish people. Think, for a moment, of your own life, and you won't have to search far for someone who was your Jewish role model and ideal. If we're lucky, we have more than one such person to illumine our lives with Torah and to warm us with the glow of Jewish living.

The stands of Jewish belonging are built one-on-one. Or, in the words of the Talmud, what comes from the heart enters the heart. However large our classes on Judaism, however magnificent our central institutions, the key component for transmitting a love of *yiddishkeit* and Torah is one Jew, willing to lavish time, caring, and wisdom on a single seeking soul.

Bradley Shavit Artson, "Sunrise, Sunset," *Learn Torah With* . . . 3, no. 5 (November 5, 1996): 1

The Journey of Spiritual Growth

Our community is strong, but have we focused too much on communal needs and too little on the needs and ambitions of the individual? Have we sent the message that an individual's hot passion for God is somehow not the concern, or even the interest, of the community? Have we forgotten that a strong community not only rescues Jewish lives but captivates Jewish souls and that there is no contradiction between Jewish community life and Jewish spiritual life? . . . The individual is the foundation of Judaism . . . and Jewish history begins with a solitary person called to God's service. It begins with Abraham, commanded to make a journey himself so that he can hear the voice of the Eternal One, find a spiritual center, and dream the dream of God.

Eric H. Yoffie, "The Never Ending Journey of Spiritual Growth," *Torat Hayim* 1, no. 3 (October 20, 1996): 4

Leading by Example: Philanthropy and Transformation

I am acutely aware that very few women, especially Jewish women, have ever been presented with the philanthropic opportunities and challenges that lay ahead of me. Nonetheless, I do not expect my gender to play a determinative role in the decisions I ultimately choose to make. I see myself as a Jewish philanthropist who happens to be a woman, not a woman philanthropist who happens to be a Jew.

Some of my earliest and fondest memories of philanthropy involve the hours I spent with my father helping to care for people I remember calling the "little old ladies." My father never talked in terms of charity. He spoke only of improving lives and, in turn, making the world a better place for all of us. Not being a religious man, he was unfamiliar with the Jewish perspective on tikkun olam or tzedakah.

After my first visit to Israel in 1977, Judaism became an essential aspect of my life rather than simply a means of self-identification. I began to define myself through my philanthropy. The groups I chose to support and the manner in which I decided to give to them became windows to my soul, clear expressions of my innermost convictions and reflections of values and traditions that were of great importance to me.

For the first time in my life, Jewish organizations and Jewish causes became the primary focus of my philanthropy. I started to devote the vast majority of my time and financial resources toward issues of Jewish concern. . . .

The challenges confronting contemporary Jewish life are so daunting that we have no time to waste on matters that divide us. Instead, we must join hands and direct our attention to issues that unite us. It is time for each of us to become Jewish philanthropists: to contribute whatever time, talent, and resources we can afford to help ensure a vibrant Jewish future.

Lynn Schusterman, "Leading by Example: Philanthropy and Transformation," *Shma.com,* April 2002, www.shma.com/Apr02/Schusterman.htm

CHAPTER SIX

ו:א יֵשׁ רָעָה אֲשֶׁר רָאִיתִי תַּחַת הַשֶּׁמֶשׁ וְרַבָּה הִיא עַל־הָאָדָם:

6:1 THERE IS AN EVIL THAT I HAVE SEEN, AND IT IS COMMON AMONG HUMANS.

Kohelet is going to present more misfortune, which is either very bad or frequent. Our translation of *rabah hi* as "common" follows Rashi. Ibn Ezra translates the word as "great."

ו:ב אִישׁ אֲשֶׁר יִתֶּן־לוֹ הָאֱלֹהִים עֹשֶׁר וּנְכָסִים וְכָבוֹד וְאֵינֶנּוּ חָסֵר לְנַפְשׁוֹ מִכֹּל אֲשֶׁר־יִתְאַוֶּה וְלֹא־יַשְׁלִיטֶנּוּ הָאֱלֹהִים לֶאֱכֹל מִמֶּנּוּ כִּי אִישׁ נָכְרִי יֹאכְלֶנּוּ זֶה הֶבֶל וָחֳלִי רָע הוּא:

6:2 GOD GIVES A PERSON WEALTH, POSSESSIONS, AND HONOR SO THAT NOTHING WILL BE LACKING, BUT THEN GOD WON'T PERMIT THAT PERSON TO ENJOY IT. INSTEAD A STRANGER IS THE ONE WHO ENJOYS IT. THIS IS A USELESS AND BAD SITUATION.

Once again, Kohelet returns to the case of a rich person without an heir or friend. The *Targum* understands the verse to mean that a person lacks nothing and yet God does not give this person the opportunity to benefit from it, while a total alien (often not even an offspring) will get the fortune. It is not clear whether Kohelet is more troubled by people's lack of enjoyment in their possessions or by the (future) enjoyment of those possessions by a stranger. From the perspective of his years of experience, this verse emphasizes Kohelet's perspective on the futility of our situation in life.

ו:ג אִם־יוֹלִיד אִישׁ מֵאָה וְשָׁנִים רַבּוֹת יִחְיֶה וְרַב שֶׁיִּהְיוּ יְמֵי־שָׁנָיו וְנַפְשׁוֹ לֹא־תִשְׂבַּע מִן־הַטּוֹבָה וְגַם־קְבוּרָה לֹא־הָיְתָה לּוֹ אָמַרְתִּי טוֹב מִמֶּנּוּ הַנָּפֶל:

6:3 IF A PERSON WERE TO BEGET ONE HUNDRED CHILDREN AND LIVE MANY YEARS, AS MANY AS THE DAYS OF ONE'S YEARS MIGHT BE, IF THAT PERSON WERE NOT TOTALLY SATISFIED AND DID NOT HAVE A PLACE OF BURIAL, THEN I SAY THAT A STILLBIRTH WOULD BE BETTER OFF.

This verse seems to be a response to the previous verse. If you can't live forever, then have children so that you can pass your fortune down to someone you know. However, while you are alive, make sure that you enjoy everything and lack for nothing, including a memorable funeral and burial plot when you die. According to Kohelet, if you don't enjoy what you have, you would have been better off not having been born.

ו:ד כִּי־בַהֶבֶל בָּא וּבַחֹשֶׁךְ יֵלֵךְ וּבַחֹשֶׁךְ שְׁמוֹ יְכֻסֶּה:

6:4 IT CAME IN VAIN AND LEFT IN DARKNESS. AND IN DARKNESS, ITS NAME WILL BE COVERED OVER.

This verse reflects traditional Jewish practices regarding stillbirths. While we might disagree with this sentiment today, according to traditional Jewish law, stillborn infants are not accorded full funeral rights nor are the parents required to follow the traditional requirements of mourning. As Ibn Ezra points out, the stillbirth's name "will be covered over" because it will not be remembered. This verse is reminiscent of Job 3:2–6, "Job spoke up and said: perish the day on which I was born, and the night it was announced, 'A male has been conceived!' May that day be darkness; may God above have no concern for it; may light not shine on it; may darkness and deep gloom reclaim it; may a pall lie over it; may what blackens the day terrify it; may obscurity carry off that night; may it not be counted among the days of the year; may it not appear in any of its months."

ו:ה גַּם־שֶׁמֶשׁ לֹא־רָאָה וְלֹא יָדָע נַחַת לָזֶה מִזֶּה:

6:5 ALTHOUGH IT NEVER SAW OR KNEW THE SUN, IT IS BETTER OFF.

Kohelet insists that nonexistence, entailing a total lack of experience, the preference of darkness over light, of no knowledge to some knowledge, is better than missing out on something that you might have had and did not get. Some may see this as the complaint of the spoiled child, however grown up that child might have been. This verse can be viewed as dark and depressing, but it may also be like a small child saying, "If I don't get my way, I am going to take my marbles and go home—and more than that, I won't come to play at all."

וּ:ו וְאִלּוּ חָיָה אֶלֶף שָׁנִים פַּעֲמַיִם וְטוֹבָה לֹא רָאָה הֲלֹא אֶל־מָקוֹם אֶחָד הַכֹּל הוֹלֵךְ:

6:6 EVEN IF ONE WERE TO LIVE A THOUSAND YEARS TWICE, AND YET NOT SEE GOODNESS, WOULD THAT PERSON NOT GO TO THE SAME PLACE WHERE ALL GO?

Kohelet contrasts the stillbirth described as *gam shemesh lo raah* (never knew the sun) of the previous verse with the long-lived person described as *v'tovah lo raah* ("and yet did not see goodness" or "and yet did not enjoy pleasure"). Kohelet makes the point that either way, both end up dead. Therefore, Kohelet concludes, it would be better to enjoy life.

וּ:ז כָּל־עֲמַל הָאָדָם לְפִיהוּ וְגַם־הַנֶּפֶשׁ לֹא תִמָּלֵא:

6:7 ALL WORK IS FOR ONE'S MOUTH, YET ONE IS NEVER SATISFIED.

The *Targum* adds the pious thought that one should have been sustained by the word of God. Some take this verse as a proverb quoted by Kohelet so that it can then be countered by the next verse.

וּ:ח כִּי מַה־יּוֹתֵר לֶחָכָם מִן־הַכְּסִיל מַה־לֶּעָנִי יוֹדֵעַ לַהֲלֹךְ נֶגֶד הַחַיִּים:

6:8 WHAT ADVANTAGE DOES A WISE PERSON HAVE OVER A FOOL OR OVER A PAUPER WHO KNOWS HOW TO PROCEED THROUGH LIFE?

Kohelet asks, how is the prudent individual better off? The last clause is problematic. The precise meaning of the phrase *yodei-a lahaloch neged hachayim* is unclear. While the individual meanings of the first three words are clear ("knows," "to walk," "in the presence of"), the meaning of *hachayim* is not clear. It can mean either, as Ibn Ezra understands it, "those who live" or "life." It is also not clear what these four words mean together. This may have been a well-known idiom whose meaning is lost to us. We have taken the phrase to mean "who knows how to proceed through life." To add to the challenge of understanding this verse correctly, it is not clear whether the phrase relates to the *ani* (pauper) or to the *chacham* (wise person). One would expect that the "wise person" would "know how to proceed through life." Some scholars suggest that the text be emended to continue the contrast between the "wise person" and the "fool" with the contrast between the "pauper" and the one who "knows how to proceed through life." Others understand the last phrase to refer to that "pauper" who at least "knows how to proceed through life." The verse is then understood to raise the question "What advantage does a wise person have?" since all people, rich or poor, wise or foolish, will never be satisfied, no matter how much work they do or energy they expend.

וּ:ט טוֹב מַרְאֵה עֵינַיִם מֵהֲלָךְ־נָפֶשׁ גַּם־זֶה הֶבֶל וּרְעוּת רוּחַ:

6:9 BETTER LOOKING AT WHAT YOU HAVE THAN YEARNING
FOR WHAT YOU DON'T HAVE. BUT THIS TOO IS USELESS
AND CHASING AFTER WIND.

This verse presents another challenge. The phrase *mareih einayim* literally means "the sight of eyes." The *Targum* translates the phrase as *ma d'it leih,* "what he has." Rashi understands the phrase as what a person sees when looking at his or her wealth, while Ibn Ezra takes the phrase as what is available to be seen. We have translated the phrase as "looking at what you have." *Meihalach nafesh* is explained by Koehler and Baumgartner (p. 246) as "desire (to wander)." Rashi takes the term to mean "to wander without knowing where one is going." Ibn Ezra takes it to mean "as what occurs to the mind." We have taken the term to mean "yearning" and have attempted to provide an idiomatic translation. Since death, no matter what we do, is the final outcome for all of us, all this planning is "useless and chasing after wind."

וּ:י מַה־שֶּׁהָיָה כְּבָר נִקְרָא שְׁמוֹ וְנוֹדָע אֲשֶׁר־הוּא אָדָם וְלֹא־יוּכַל לָדִין
עִם שהתקיף שֶׁתַּקִּיף מִמֶּנּוּ:

6:10 WHATEVER HAPPENS HAS ALREADY BEEN DESTINED
AND IS KNOWN; NO HUMAN CAN CONTEND WITH ONE
WHO IS STRONGER.

The *Targum* understands *adam* (human) as Adam. Whether Adam or any of his (and Eve's) descendants, no human can argue with God, who is omnipotent.

וּ:יא כִּי יֵשׁ־דְּבָרִים הַרְבֵּה מַרְבִּים הָבֶל מַה־יֹּתֵר לָאָדָם:

6:11 MANY WORDS MULTIPLY FUTILITY. WHAT GAIN CAN
THERE BE FOR ANYONE?

If one cannot contend with power, what good are words, whether few or many? Life is short. Why waste time on that which is useless? Rashi takes the word *d'varim* to mean "things" and relates the first clause to what he thinks have no clear purpose, like monkeys, elephants, and lions.

וּ:יב כִּי מִי־יוֹדֵעַ מַה־טוֹב לָאָדָם בַּחַיִּים מִסְפַּר יְמֵי־חַיֵּי הֶבְלוֹ וְיַעֲשֵׂם כַּצֵּל אֲשֶׁר מִי־יַגִּיד לָאָדָם מַה־יִּהְיֶה אַחֲרָיו תַּחַת הַשָּׁמֶשׁ:

6:12 WHO KNOWS WHAT IS GOOD FOR ANYONE TO DO IN LIFE, IN THE NUMBERED DAYS OF A FLEETING LIFE, WHICH BECOMES LIKE A SHADOW? WHO CAN TELL ANYONE WHAT WILL BE FOR THAT PERSON UNDER THE SUN?

The phrase *v'yaaseim katzeil* may be translated literally as "and he made them like a shadow." The *Targum* understands the phrase as *inun chashivin b'einoy kitlala*, "they are considered in his eyes like a shadow." For Rashi, the phrase refers to the short period that one is alive, which passes like the shadow of a bird flying into and out of sight.

Mourning Practices Regarding Children

Because of what is written in the *Shulchan Aruch*, people assume that infants who have not survived thirty days *cannot* be afforded full Jewish burial rites. While that has been the prevailing custom, parents are not *prohibited* from doing so. Therefore, one might go beyond the halachah and give them full rites. Babies who survive beyond the fifth month are to be buried in the sanctified grounds of a Jewish cemetery. More and more rabbis encourage parents to take advantage of Jewish mourning rituals, which help parents cope with their tragic loss in a spiritually sound manner and help them on the road to healing.

Free Will

If God is omniscient and knows everything, then does the human have free will? This conundrum has perplexed Jewish thinkers for centuries. For if God knows everything and humans do not have free will, how can they be held responsible (and therefore punished) for their actions? Thus, classic philosophers have held that humans do have free will and God knows what choices humans will make. As a result, they are held responsible for their actions. Some contemporary Jewish thinkers argue that God's power is limited and that God cannot know everything and cannot intervene in human affairs of the workings of nature.

GLEANINGS

Engaging the Words of Torah

As a 3,000-year-old religious tradition, Judaism has a depth and richness that doesn't generally whitewash reality; our greatest leaders are presented in all their nasty humanness. As in any authentic, committed relationship, I take the good with the bad. If I cannot always accept all aspects of the tradition, at least I have found equanimity in my response. If I felt only negative responses to my Jewish heritage, then I would need to leave (and probably become a pagan or a Buddhist like so many of my contemporaries). A college friend of mine used to call this the "yum to yuch ratio." His theory was that a good relationship had a yum to yuch ratio of at least three to one. Happily, I can report that Torah and Judaism meets this test for me.

A voice within me resists measuring this relationship in yums to yuchs. Torah is a sacred covenant, a committed relationship. The depth of my commitment to Judaism and Torah empowers me to be touched deeply and take risks. Judaism teaches that redemption is possible—my own redemption, that of my tradition, and that of the world. My experiences of rage and grief, rationalization, equanimity—even denial—can be redemptive and transformative. That which I find most disturbing pushes me toward constructive change.

Jane Rachel Littman, "Working with the Words of Torah," Sh'ma 31/579 (April 2001): 3

Free Will

There is an inescapable dialectic in Jewish thought with which each generation of Jews has struggled. How can we reconcile God's providence with our own free will? This is, of course, one of the classic problems of theology. The Bible is full of examples of God determining the destiny of nations and individuals. Yet, free will is at the core of what it means to be a human being. The dialectical nature of free will and God's providence is seen from the very beginning of the Torah. Adam and Eve freely choose to disobey God by eating from the forbidden tree. As a result, they are punished and exiled from the garden. However, that exile is in itself a necessary part of God's divine plan.

The Rabbinic tradition tried to articulate a position that balanced God's providence with the centrality of free will. Rabbi Akiba's statement in the Ethics of the Fathers sums it up: "All is foreseen, but freedom of choice is given." While we are free to choose, what we will choose is already woven into a divine plan of which we are unaware at the time of our choosing. The Talmud had an even more complex way of summing up this dialectic: "Everything is in the hands of heaven except the fear of heaven." This statement might mean that while much is determined in our lives by God's providence, our own degree of reverence expressed through the choices we make determine outcomes that God does not control.

Leon A. Morris, "Parashat Vayigash," eTorah, 2 January 2001, 1

Happiness, Love, and Wisdom

Once a woman dreamed that she walked into a store and found God standing behind the counter. God said to her, "You can have anything your heart desires, just wish for it."

"I want happiness, love, and wisdom," said the woman.

God looked at her and said, "I don't think you understand. I can give you only seeds. Whether they become flowers is up to you."

Byron L. Sherwin, *Why Be Good? Seeking Our Best Selves in a Challenging World*
(New York: Daybreak Books, 1998), 181

The Double-Edged Sword of Will

The triumphalism of the will ignores what wisdom understands: the limitations of will. I can will my smile—I cannot will my happiness. I can will my eating, I cannot will my hunger. I can will going to sleep, I cannot will my dreams. I can will knowledge, I cannot will wisdom. I can will my self-assertion, I cannot will my courage. I can will shaving, combing, dressing up—I cannot will my joy. I can will purchasing flowers, perfume, candies—I cannot will love. I can will fasting, the recitation of the litany of transgressions—I cannot will remorse. I can will opening the prayer book and Bible—I cannot will belief. "A wink is not a blink." One I will, one I do not. I can will many things, but I cannot will my will.

Harold M. Schulweis, "Conversation with the Angel of Death"
(Rosh HaShanah sermon, Valley Beth Shalom, Encino, Calif., 1991), 4–5.

CHAPTER SEVEN

ז:א טוֹב שֵׁם מִשֶּׁמֶן טוֹב וְיוֹם הַמָּוֶת מִיּוֹם הִוָּלְדוֹ:

7:1 A GOOD NAME IS BETTER THAN FINE OIL, AND THE
DAY OF DEATH IS BETTER THAN THE DAY OF BIRTH.

Shemen tov usually refers to a cosmetic or an expensive perfume. As a result, it is
assumed that such perfume was not used by the general population. *Shem* (name)
and *shemen* (oil) are a play on words. According to the *Targum,* the ''oil'' in this verse
refers to anointing oil that is used to consecrate kings and priests. Thus, a good name
(that is, a good reputation), achieved by the righteous in this world, is greater than
the oil that is symbolic of the highest status. Having achieved merit in the course of
their lives, the righteous will be at a higher level at death than they were at birth.
For Rashi, the comparison between oil and a good name is due to a parallel in their
natures. Oil, unlike other liquids, is difficult to corrupt because it does not mix with
lesser liquids. Similarly, a good name (a good reputation) reflects the total goodness of
the person so described. For Ibn Ezra, the ''oil'' is symbolic of wealth, while ''a good
name'' is symbolic of the merit that a person who is righteous may achieve even
though he or she may be poor. Kohelet says it rather simply: everyone has the
possibility of forfeiting a good name until the day of death. When you are born, no
one knows what you will accomplish, but at the end of life, your accomplishments
have all been concluded. Thus, anyone can surmise what kind of person you were by
what you did.

ז:ב טוֹב לָלֶכֶת אֶל־בֵּית־אֵבֶל מִלֶּכֶת אֶל־בֵּית מִשְׁתֶּה בַּאֲשֶׁר הוּא
סוֹף כָּל־הָאָדָם וְהַחַי יִתֵּן אֶל־לִבּוֹ:

7:2 IT IS BETTER TO GO TO A HOUSE OF MOURNING THAN
TO A TAVERN, FOR EVERY HUMAN BEING ENDS THERE
[IN THE HOUSE OF MOURNING]. LET EVERYONE ALIVE
PAY ATTENTION.

This is a rather morose verse, the kind of dark Kohelet sentiment to which the reader
has become accustomed. Kohelet reminds us of what we often hide from ourselves—
the very fact that we, as humans, are mortal. The contrast between *beit eivel* (house of
mourning) and *beit mishteh* (literally, ''house of drinking''; a banquet or tavern)
should remind us that alcohol is often used as a means of self-concealment. Perhaps
Kohelet is quoting a familiar proverb or reflecting on his own life. His message is
straightforward: knowing life is finite, reconsider what your life is all about.

זָ:ג טוֹב כַּעַס מִשְׂחֹק כִּי־בְרֹעַ פָּנִים יִיטַב לֵב:

7:3 ANGER IS BETTER THAN LAUGHTER. ONE CAN APPEAR
TROUBLED AND YET BE HAPPY.

However this verse is translated, it is difficult to translate. *Kaas* is translated by some
people as "vexation." Others translate it as "sorrow" or "anger." The *Targum*
translates it as "anger." We have done so as well, because both laughter and anger
are specific human behaviors and Kohelet's proverbs, whether chosen or composed
by him, deal with the human condition. The last two words of the verse, *yitav lev,*
form an idiom that means "be happy." This idiom can also be found where it is used
similarly in I Kings 8:66: "They bade the king good-bye and went to their homes,
joyful and glad of heart. . . ." The point of the last clause seems to be clear: it is easier
to look angry and not be angry than to laugh and be angry. This verse provides
Ibn Ezra with a platform to make a long philosophical dissertation on the human soul.
According to him (and others, such as Saadyah Gaon, whom he quotes), the soul has
three elements: vegetative, animal, and rational. These three elements, which are
sometimes called souls themselves rather than parts of them, are united and act as
one entity. The three different names reflect their different faculties and operations:
nefesh reflects desire; *ruach* reflects anger; and *n'shamah* reflects thought.

זָ:ד לֵב חֲכָמִים בְּבֵית אֵבֶל וְלֵב כְּסִילִים בְּבֵית שִׂמְחָה:

7:4 THE MIND OF THE WISE IS IN THE HOUSE OF
MOURNING. THE MIND OF THE FOOLS IS IN THE
HOUSE OF MIRTH.

The verse seems to say that wherever they are, the wise think about mortality and
the limitations of the human condition, while fools seek only personal enjoyment
and pleasure. The *Targum* relates the verse to the destruction of the Temple: the
wise mourn and reflect on its destruction, while the fools are indifferent and engage
in irresponsible behavior. Those who really understand know what life is all about.
The others are superficial. Rashi relates the verse to the day of death: the wise reflect
on it, and fools are indifferent to it. Ibn Ezra says that the wise always reflect on
their death. Perhaps Kohelet is recommending that we focus on death in order
to appreciate the days we are alive. Such a perspective would then be consistent
with *Kohelet* 2:24, from which this teaching would have emerged naturally.
Or perhaps, from the perspective of old age, Kohelet has simply changed his mind.
If so, then 2:24 contradicts this verse, which may be why, in his comment on the
previous verse, Ibn Ezra reminds the reader that the Rabbis sought to suppress
this book because they felt that its verses (and therefore its teachings) included
inherent contradictions.

ז:ה טוֹב לִשְׁמֹעַ גַּעֲרַת חָכָם מֵאִישׁ שֹׁמֵעַ שִׁיר כְּסִילִים:

7:5 IT IS BETTER TO HEAR THE REPROACH OF THE WISE
THAN THE SONG OF THE FOOLISH.

It is not a far stretch to connect "fools" with "singing" and "drinking." The connection between drinking and singing is established in Isaiah 24:9, where "they drink their wine without song" is used as an example of a time devoid of joy. Having been warned about a *beit mishteh* (house of drinking, a tavern) in 7:2 and having been told that only "fools" go to a *beit simchah* (house of mirth) in 7:4, it is not surprising here to read a negative view of "the song of the foolish." The wise who gather in a house of mourning to reflect on death and the meaning of life can reprove one another or be reproved. Fools who are indifferent to death are motivated to sing and just "be happy." Maybe the fools are singing another famous line from Isaiah (22:13), "Eat and drink, for tomorrow we die!"

ז:ו כִּי כְקוֹל הַסִּירִים תַּחַת הַסִּיר כֵּן שְׂחֹק הַכְּסִיל וְגַם־זֶה הָבֶל:

7:6 LIKE THE SOUND OF THORNS CRACKLING BENEATH
A POT, SO IS THE SOUND OF A FOOL. BUT THIS TOO
IS USELESS.

There is a play on words in this verse: *sirim* (thorns) and *sir* (pot). The verse presents this image: the meaningless sounds of thorns crackling as they burn beneath the pot is like the meaningless discourse of fools. There may be another play on words, as well. The previous verse contained *shir k'silim* (song of fools); this verse includes *kol hasirim* (the voice of fools). With all the differences between the wise and the foolish, one thing remains certain: both will die. The wise words of one group and the foolish words of the other will all sink into oblivion.

ז:ז כִּי הָעֹשֶׁק יְהוֹלֵל חָכָם וִיאַבֵּד אֶת־לֵב מַתָּנָה:

7:7 FOR EXTORTION MAY DRIVE A WISE PERSON MAD, AND
A GIFT MAY DESTROY UNDERSTANDING.

Kohelet is referring to a familiar truism: money talks. The threat of its loss or the possibility of its gain affects how people think. Often, wealth makes a fool out of the wise. Extortion and bribery would not be effective criminal tools were people not affected by money.

ז:ח טוֹב אַחֲרִית דָּבָר מֵרֵאשִׁיתוֹ טוֹב אֶרֶךְ־רוּחַ מִגְּבַהּ־רוּחַ:

7:8 THE END OF THE MATTER IS BETTER THAN ITS
BEGINNING. PATIENCE IS BETTER THAN PRIDE.

Kohelet may be reciting a proverb in this verse, since he seems to be presenting a common truism. Rashi provides a simple interpretation, as well as a profound one. He says that at the beginning of any matter, one cannot tell how it will turn out. But one does know at its conclusion. He then quotes the midrash (*Kohelet Rabbah* 7:18) that refers the verse to the deathbed repentance of the heretic Elisha ben Abuyah. Ibn Ezra refers the verse to the thought and action of the wise. He offers an example: the wise person knows that taking foul-tasting medicine may be better in the long run than taking medicine that tastes sweet.

ז:ט אַל־תְּבַהֵל בְּרוּחֲךָ לִכְעוֹס כִּי כַעַס בְּחֵיק כְּסִילִים יָנוּחַ:

7:9 DON'T BE TOO QUICK TO GET ANGRY, FOR ANGER
RESTS IN THE BOSOM OF FOOLS.

This also may be a proverb quoted by Kohelet. Perhaps it is something that he wrote down earlier in his life and made it his own. Or perhaps it was something that he offers from the perspective of old age. There is a similar notion, presented with different words, in Proverbs 19:11: "One's intelligence is manifest in one's patience, one's glory in one's forgiveness of offense." Wisdom calls on individuals to control their behavior, especially their anger.

ז:י אַל־תֹּאמַר מֶה הָיָה שֶׁהַיָּמִים הָרִאשֹׁנִים הָיוּ טוֹבִים מֵאֵלֶּה כִּי לֹא מֵחָכְמָה שָׁאַלְתָּ עַל־זֶה:

7:10 DON'T SAY: HOW IS IT THAT THE OLD DAYS WERE
BETTER THAN THESE DAYS? THAT'S NOT A SMART
QUESTION.

Our tendency to glorify the past is part of the process of selective memory. Even during their journey toward freedom in the desert, the Israelites looked back at Egypt as a place of unlimited and varied food, forgetting that it was the place of their enslavement (see Exodus 16:3ff. and Numbers 11:4ff.). In this verse, there is an implicit assumption that the earlier days were no better. As a statement of humility, the Rabbis always assumed that pervious generations knew more than their own. Perhaps it was because the closer you are to Sinai, the closer you are to the reality of God's miracles and can speak authentically about them.

ז:יא טוֹבָה חָכְמָה עִם־נַחֲלָה וְיֹתֵר לְרֹאֵי הַשָּׁמֶשׁ׃

7:11 Wisdom is better with an inheritance, a benefit
to all who see the sun.

The *Targum* understands the ''wisdom'' to be *d'oraita* (of the Torah) and the
''inheritance'' to be *mamonah* (money). For Rashi, the ''wisdom'' is the wisdom of
the Torah, while the ''inheritance'' is *z'chut avotam* (the merit of the ancestors).
For Ibn Ezra, ''wisdom'' is the immortal form of the soul.

ז:יב כִּי בְּצֵל הַחָכְמָה בְּצֵל הַכָּסֶף וְיִתְרוֹן דַּעַת הַחָכְמָה תְּחַיֶּה בְעָלֶיהָ׃

7:12 For the shelter of wisdom is the shelter of
money, but the advantage of knowing wisdom
is that it preserves those who possess it.

As the *Targum,* Rashi, and Ibn Ezra agree, ''wisdom'' transcends death; money does
not. Once again, the *Targum* and Rashi emphasize that ''wisdom'' is the Torah.
For Ibn Ezra, it is philosophy.

ז:יג רְאֵה אֶת־מַעֲשֵׂה הָאֱלֹהִים כִּי מִי יוּכַל לְתַקֵּן אֵת אֲשֶׁר עִוְּתוֹ׃

7:13 Look at the work of God! Who can straighten
what has been bent?

Rashi takes the first clause to refer to God's handiwork in creating *Gan Eden* (paradise)
for the righteous and *Geihinom* (hell) for the wicked. The *Targum* takes the second
clause to refer to God and understands ''what has been bent'' as those whom
the Divine has created with various handicaps, such as the *samya* (blind), *g'vinah*
(those lacking eyebrows), and *chagira* (those whose mobility is limited). Rashi
takes the second clause to refer to the individual's situation after death, without
repentance. At that point, no one can straighten out the individual's errant ways.
Perhaps Ibn Ezra was reflecting on his personal plight when he suggested that the
verse refers to a wise person who lacks wealth. That person should not fret about his
or her economic fate. It is a function of the array of constellations, sealed from the six
days of Creation.

זיד בְּיוֹם טוֹבָה הֱיֵה בְטוֹב וּבְיוֹם רָעָה רְאֵה גַּם אֶת־זֶה לְעֻמַּת־זֶה
עָשָׂה הָאֱלֹהִים עַל־דִּבְרַת שֶׁלֹּא יִמְצָא הָאָדָם אַחֲרָיו מְאוּמָה:

7:14 ON A DAY OF GOOD FORTUNE, ENJOY IT. ON A DAY OF
MISFORTUNE, THINK! GOD HAS MADE ONE AS WELL AS
THE OTHER SO THAT NO INDIVIDUAL CAN LODGE A
COMPLAINT AGAINST THE DIVINE.

The *Targum*, Rashi, and Ibn Ezra all take the phrase *shelo yimtzah haadam acharav
m'umah* (literally, "that a person may not find any matter after him") to mean that
"no one can complain against God." Kohelet seems to say that since both good and
evil come from God, you must enjoy the good and accept the bad.

זיטו אֶת־הַכֹּל רָאִיתִי בִּימֵי הֶבְלִי יֵשׁ צַדִּיק אֹבֵד בְּצִדְקוֹ וְיֵשׁ רָשָׁע
מַאֲרִיךְ בְּרָעָתוֹ:

7:15 I HAVE SEEN IT ALL IN MY USELESS DAYS: AN INNOCENT
PERSON DESTROYED, THOUGH INNOCENT, AND A
GUILTY PERSON LONG-LIVED, THOUGH EVIL.

Kohelet challenges the view that virtuous people are rewarded with long lives while
those who do evil are punished with an early death. Our experience often confirms
what Kohelet learned in his life: there is no correlation between virtue and its reward
and wrongdoing and its punishment. However, we must acknowledge that we can
never really know God's way. Often there are reasons for events that occur that are
simply beyond our human ability to comprehend. The *Targum* has an explanation
for such disparate fates for people: it is *al eisak mazalya*, "due to the array of the
constellations under which people were born." Ibn Ezra understands the phrase *oveid
b'tzidko*, "perishing though innocent," as "perishing because of one's innocence,"
that is, a person who ruins one's health by continuous fasting.

זיטז אַל־תְּהִי צַדִּיק הַרְבֵּה וְאַל־תִּתְחַכַּם יוֹתֵר לָמָּה תִּשּׁוֹמֵם:

7:16 THEREFORE, DON'T BE SO INNOCENT AND DON'T BE
SO SMART. WHY RUIN YOURSELF?

Do not be overly wise. Do not regard yourself as all-knowing. Realize that you too
have your faults, even at your very best. Do not be self-righteous. Ibn Ezra
understands the verse as a warning against excess. If one were to pray from morning
until night and to fast continually, such a person might end up turning away from a
normal life and be ruined. He offers as an example hermits who live among Christians
and Moslems.

ז:יז אַל־תִּרְשַׁע הַרְבֵּה וְאַל־תְּהִי סָכָל לָמָּה תָמוּת בְּלֹא עִתֶּךָ:

7:17 Don't get too guilty and don't be a fool. Why should you die before your time?

In this verse, Kohelet seems to be teaching the opposite of what he taught in the previous verse. Perhaps this is the understanding that he came to in his old age, now rejecting what he learned while younger, as reflected in the previous verse. Perhaps it simply means that all wickedness is in overdoing. Ibn Ezra notes that most acts of wickedness put their perpetrators at risk. While the term will not be used for a thousand years after Kohelet, Kohelet seems to be arguing for a "golden mean" of sorts, a middle position between two extremes.

ז:יח טוֹב אֲשֶׁר תֶּאֱחֹז בָּזֶה וְגַם־מִזֶּה אַל־תַּנַּח אֶת־יָדֶךָ כִּי־יְרֵא אֱלֹהִים יֵצֵא אֶת־כֻּלָּם:

7:18 It is good to hold on to the one and not let go of the other, for the one who fears God will fulfill all.

From the context, it would seem that "the one" and "the other" are related to the examples in the verses above that offer two types of behaviors. Kohelet's message appears to be: "Don't be too good" and "Don't be too bad." He seems to be advocating a "golden mean" in this verse as well. There is being good by not being bad and being good by overcoming bad. So do not regard yourself as altogether honest or good.

ז:יט הַחָכְמָה תָּעֹז לֶחָכָם מֵעֲשָׂרָה שַׁלִּיטִים אֲשֶׁר הָיוּ בָּעִיר:

7:19 Wisdom provides more strength to a wise person than ten rulers can give to a city.

Wisdom is more of a defense for the righteous than any ten members of the aristocracy in a city. This seems to be another proverb quoted by Kohelet, unrelated to the verses that proceed or follow. The *Targum* applies the verse to Joseph and the "ten rulers" to his brothers, excluding Benjamin. Rashi takes the first clause as a reference to repentance and the second clause as a reference to the meritorious acts of King Josiah (II Kings 23:25). Rashi also takes this second clause as a kind of parable that relates to the ten parts of the body—the hands, the eyes, the ears, the feet, the heart, and the mouth—which may lead a person to sin. Similarly, he takes it as a parable of aspects of the digestive process. Having presented a variety of midrashim, Rashi confesses that he cannot relate any of them to the following verse.

ז:כ כִּי אָדָם אֵין צַדִּיק בָּאָרֶץ אֲשֶׁר יַעֲשֶׂה־טּוֹב וְלֹא יֶחֱטָא:

7:20 FOR THERE IS NO PERSON ON EARTH SO RIGHTEOUS
WHO DOES GOOD AND NEVER SINS.

Had this been placed after verse 18, it might have been more easily connected. The *Targum* takes the verse as it is—and where it is—and adds a word of advice: a person so described should repent. Rashi suggests that such people should examine their deeds as a preparation for repentance. Ibn Ezra relates this to verse 16.

ז:כא גַּם לְכָל־הַדְּבָרִים אֲשֶׁר יְדַבֵּרוּ אַל־תִּתֵּן לִבֶּךָ אֲשֶׁר לֹא־תִשְׁמַע
אֶת־עַבְדְּךָ מְקַלְלֶךָ:

7:21 PAY NO ATTENTION TO THE WORDS THAT PEOPLE SAY.
THAT WAY, YOU WON'T HEAR YOUR SERVANT CURSE
YOU.

We have translated *m'kal'lecha* as "curse you" with the sense of the America slang "cuss you out" rather than invoking the Deity against a person. This verse seems to be another proverb quoted by Kohelet or something he wrote down in his "diary" and quoted throughout his life. Its point is clear: if you don't listen to what others say, you can't be hurt by their words. Paying attention to such words, Ibn Ezra warns, negatively affects the apprehension of wisdom.

ז:כב כִּי גַּם־פְּעָמִים רַבּוֹת יָדַע לִבֶּךָ אֲשֶׁר גַּם־אַתָּ קִלַּלְתָּ אֲחֵרִים:

7:22 YOU KNOW VERY WELL THE MANY TIMES YOU HAVE
CURSED OTHER PEOPLE.

The message of this verse is unclear. Individuals know how often they "bad-mouth" others. Often they do not think it bad at the time they are doing it. Perhaps the verse means that having reviled others, you deserve to be reviled, even by one far beneath your socioeconomic class. Thus, the ultimate message is: Don't revile anyone. Alternatively, the message is: Pay no attention to anything that anyone says, since most of what is said has no effect. After all, you were not harmed by what your servant says, and others were not harmed by what you said.

ז:כג כָּל־זֹה נִסִּיתִי בַחָכְמָה אָמַרְתִּי אֶחְכָּמָה וְהִיא רְחוֹקָה מִמֶּנִּי:

7:23 I TESTED EVERYTHING IN WISDOM, THINKING THAT
I COULD BECOME WISE, BUT IT WAS BEYOND ME.

Kohelet put everything to the test of reason. As the next verse indicates, by "wisdom" Kohelet means the entire realm of human inquiry. As might be expected, the *Targum* and Rashi take "wisdom" to refer to the Torah. Ibn Ezra connects this with verse 16.

ז:כד רָחוֹק מַה־שֶּׁהָיָה וְעָמֹק עָמֹק מִי יִמְצָאֶנּוּ:

7:24 WHAT HAS OCCURRED IS BEYOND US AND SO VERY DEEP, WHO CAN FIND IT?

No matter how much I question and reason, it is beyond me. The *Targum* translation reads *ha k'var itrachek mibnei n'sha l'meida kol mah dahavah min yomei alma,* "it is far from people to know what occurred from the days of old." Rashi understands the first clause as referring to all things that have occurred from the first days of Creation. Kohelet presents the reader with a paradox: he thinks that ultimate wisdom is beyond human capacity; however, as the next verse indicates, he will make an attempt to learn what can be learned.

ז:כה סַבּוֹתִי אֲנִי וְלִבִּי לָדַעַת וְלָתוּר וּבַקֵּשׁ חָכְמָה וְחֶשְׁבּוֹן וְלָדַעַת רֶשַׁע כֶּסֶל וְהַסִּכְלוּת הוֹלֵלוֹת:

7:25 SO I DIRECTED MY MIND TO STUDY, TO EXPLORE, AND TO SEEK WISDOM AND RECKONING, AND TO STUDY EVIL, FOLLY, STUPIDITY, AND MADNESS.

Cheshbon (reckoning) in later Hebrew came to mean "calculation." Hence, the *Targum* applies the term to the calculation *v'chushban agar ovadoi d'tzadikaya,* "the calculation of the reward for the deeds of the righteous." Rashi applies the term to *keitz hageulah,* "the date of the Redemption." Ibn Ezra translates the term as *machshevet hadaat,* "the process of thought." Kohelet declares that he has studied every aspect and every extreme of human thought.

ז:כו וּמוֹצֶא אֲנִי מַר מִמָּוֶת אֶת־הָאִשָּׁה אֲשֶׁר־הִיא מְצוֹדִים וַחֲרָמִים לִבָּהּ אֲסוּרִים יָדֶיהָ טוֹב לִפְנֵי הָאֱלֹהִים יִמָּלֵט מִמֶּנָּה וְחוֹטֵא יִלָּכֶד בָּהּ:

7:26 AND I DISCOVERED THAT A WOMAN IS MORE BITTER THAN DEATH. SHE IS A TRAP. HER HEART IS A SNARE. HER HANDS ARE CHAINS. THE ONE WHO HAS GOD'S FAVOR GETS AWAY FROM HER, BUT THE ONE WHO LACKS IT IS CAUGHT BY HER.

It is a disappointment that after all of his study and reflection, Kohelet has learned to be a misogynist. While some editors may choose to translate this verse using terms that are more gender sensitive, we felt it was important to communicate Kohelet's sentiments, even if we disagree with them. Kohelet never confronted women as his equals. Although *Eishet Chayil* (Proverbs 31:10–31, "A Woman of Valor," read at Friday evening dinner) certainly presented a woman as equal to a man in the economic sphere, a king (and Kohelet claimed to be a king) would not have dealt with tradespeople. The only women a king would have dealt with, other than those in his immediate family, were concubines and women of the court. One should keep in mind, too, that this is a connection between courtesans and women of the court! The context suggests that *chotei* (sinner) is not meant literally. Hence it is translated as "the one who lacks it" (that is, God's favor). Rashi softens the impact of the verse by taking "woman" as a parable for *epikursus* (heresy). Perhaps out of his own personal experience, Ibn Ezra takes the verse literally and explains that sexual desire can blind the eyes of the wise and corrupt their thought. As in Proverbs 6:24–34 (and elsewhere in some literature), woman is portrayed as temptation itself, a threat to thought and a danger to life.

ז:כז רְאֵה זֶה מָצָאתִי אָמְרָה קֹהֶלֶת אַחַת לְאַחַת לִמְצֹא חֶשְׁבּוֹן:

7:27 LOOK, THIS IS WHAT I HAVE DISCOVERED, SAYS KOHELET, AS ONE BY ONE, I SOUGHT TO FIND A REASON.

Ibn Ezra suggests that this verse is linked to the next one. If this is the case, then *achat l'achat* (one by one) may mean "one woman after another" and may refer to Kohelet's search to find the right woman. The context of the verse suggests strongly that the later, postbiblical meaning of *cheshbon* as "list," "accounting," or "bill" fits here. Perhaps Kohelet has made up a list of women, presenting one after another, until he finds the right one.

ז:כח אֲשֶׁר עוֹד־בִּקְשָׁה נַפְשִׁי וְלֹא מָצָאתִי אָדָם אֶחָד מֵאֶלֶף מָצָאתִי וְאִשָּׁה בְכָל־אֵלֶּה לֹא מָצָאתִי:

7:28 THUS, WHAT I REALLY WANTED, I NEVER FOUND: ONE MAN AMONG A THOUSAND I COULD FIND, BUT NOT A WOMAN AMONG THAT MANY.

Based on the interpretation that what was searched for was someone imbued with wisdom, this can be read as stating that there is only one *chacham* (wise person) in a thousand people. Some may read this as "and it is never a woman" or "and he is never with a woman." As an explanation, Rashi adds to Kohelet's archaic view of women and calls our attention to the rabbinic statement *kulan daatan kalah aleihen,* "all [women's] minds are flighty."

ז:כט לְבַד רְאֵה־זֶה מָצָאתִי אֲשֶׁר עָשָׂה הָאֱלֹהִים אֶת־הָאָדָם יָשָׁר
וְהֵמָּה בִקְשׁוּ חִשְּׁבֹנוֹת רַבִּים:

7:29 BESIDES, LOOK WHAT I HAVE DISCOVERED: GOD MADE
PEOPLE HONEST, BUT THEY HAVE LOOKED FOR MANY
SCHEMES.

Kohelet's struggle is futile. He cannot know what he is seeking to know. The *Targum*
and Rashi take *haadam* (the man, the person, people) to refer to Adam. "They" then
refers to Adam and Eve once they had eaten from the fruit of the Tree of Knowledge
of Good and Evil. We followed Rashi's interpretation of *chishvonot* as *mezimot*
(schemes). Ibn Ezra connects this verse with the previous one and understands
haadam as "men" and "they" referring to women in general. The only discrepancy in
the interpretations of *haadam* between the *Targum*, Rashi, and Ibn Ezra is whether to
place blame on one woman or all women.

Saadyah Gaon

Saadyah ben Joseph from Fayyum in Egypt (882–942) is considered by most to be the
father of medieval Jewish philosophy. He was the first to develop the notions of Islamic
theology and philosophy in an independent manner. Similarly, he was the first to
develop a philosophic justification for Judaism. He received his training in Egypt, where
he lived the first thirty years of his life. He subsequently lived in the Land of Israel,
Syria, and Babylonia. In 928, he became the *gaon* (head) of the well-known rabbinical
academy in Sura, Babylonia.

Saadyah was also a pioneer in Hebrew philology. He translated the Bible into Arabic,
and his commentaries on it laid the foundation for a scientific interpretation of the
Bible. Much of his extensive literary output focused on polemics against Karaism.
His entire system of philosophy can be found in his *Book of Beliefs and Opinions*.
Saadyah's doctrine concerning the relationship between reason and revelation—which
was accepted by most subsequent Jewish philosophers—provided the methodological
foundation for his religious philosophy. For him, religious truth, a distinct form of
truth, is found in revelation. Reason provides the common foundation for all religions.
For Saadyah, only Judaism is the work of God; all others were developed by humankind
and therefore falsely claim divine origin.

Aspects of the Soul

The Greek philosopher Plato (427–347 B.C.E.) taught that the human soul has three
parts: reason or mind, spirit, and desire. Since spirit and desire were linked to the body,
they could not transcend death as could the mind, which was not so linked. Aristotle
(384–322 B.C.E.), on the other hand, contended that the three parts of the human soul
related to different functions of the body. Galen (129–199 C.E.), physician and

philosopher, carried on Plato's threefold division of the soul. Thinkers in the Middle Ages understood him to believe that there were either three souls or one soul that operated on three levels. While Maimonides argued that the soul is what distinguishes between what is alive and what is not, he believed that each soul may be divided into three sections that are loosely based on the major functions of each division, which he named vegetative, animal, and rational.

Elisha ben Abuyah

Living in the second century, Elisha ben Abuyah was a teacher of Rabbi Meir. His teachings focused more on ethical behaviors, because he contended that without an ethical foundation, following the letter of the law has no value. He later rejected Rabbinic Judaism, particularly the pivotal principles of reward and punishment and resurrection of the dead. Ben Abuyah probably felt dejected after the failure of the Bar Kochba rebellion and was influenced heavily by mystical thought. Rabbinic literature often refers to him as *acher* (the other). *As a Driven Leaf* is an excellent historical novel focusing on his life, written by Milton Steinberg.

Kohelet Rabbah

Kohelet Rabbah refers to a midrash written on the Book of Ecclesiastes in the Land of Israel. It was called *Midrash Kohelet* or *Haggadat Kohelet* in the Middle Ages. Sometimes it was referred to as *Midrash Chazita*. The midrash covers nearly every verse of the Book of *Kohelet* and is divided into three relatively uneven sections. The volume draws a large portion of its material from prior collections, most notably the midrash on Genesis and Leviticus. While material from an earlier period is included, the collection dates to the seventh century C.E.

Z'chut Avot *(Merit of the Ancestors)*

Z'chut avot generally refers to the traditional doctrine that the pious deeds of one's parents secure blessings for one's children. In the Torah, we see evidence of it in the giving of the Ten Commandments, in which God "shows kindness to the thousandth generation of those who love Me and keep My commandments" (Exodus 20:6). According to the Rabbis in the midrash, the idea of *z'chut avot* has particular relevance with regard to our blessings that are dependent on the good deeds of the Patriarchs. During the Middle Ages, the idea developed that the deeds of children—particularly through a pious life and prayer—could bring blessing to deceased parents.

Gan Eden *(Paradise) and* Geihinom *(Hell), and the Soul's Immortality*

During the period of the Second Temple, there appears to have been a brief discussion about the immortality of the soul, as can be seen in the Books of the Maccabees. While there are a variety of opinions expressed about the end of life, immortality, and "heaven and hell" in the Talmud and midrash, they are not presented in any kind of system. Rabbinic doctrine emphasizes the existence of a world-to-come because it is in that world (and not necessarily our own) that a person will be resurrected, and the righteous will be rewarded while the wicked are punished. According to the Talmud (*Shabbat* 152a), after a person dies, the soul leaves the body but retains a temporary relationship with it for twelve months, until the body has fully disintegrated. Some say that the righteous go to paradise (*Gan Eden*) and the wicked go to hell (*Geihinom*) after this period. It is rather unclear what is the state of the soul during this period of time. During the messianic period of redemption, the soul will be returned to the body as the individual is resurrected. The messianic redemption is both politically and physically utopian. At the end of the period of redemption is the world-to-come, where the righteous sit in the blissful presence of the Divine.

Golden Mean

Although the use of the term "golden mean" first occurred in 1587, the notion of moderation and the balancing of extremes as an ethical goal first occurs in Artistotle's *Ethics.* From the *Ethics,* Maimonides takes the notion into his *Sh'monah P'rakim* (Eight Chapters), the introduction to his commentary on *Pirkei Avot.* Maimonides presents a kind of behavioral therapy: since the mean between the extremes is the ideal, people who have moved from the mean, misers, for example, are brought back to the mean by moving them in the opposite direction by training them for a period to act as spendthrifts. Hopefully, after such therapy, the former miser will be moved to the mean and will be neither miser nor spendthrift.

King Josiah

Reigning as the king of Judah (640–609 B.C.E.), Josiah ascended the throne at the age of eight following the assassination of his father, Amon. Josiah strengthened Judah. Taking advantage of the deteriorating Assyrian empire, he expanded Judah's frontiers to the north to include almost all of what was formerly the Northern Kingdom of Israel. His most important contribution was the reform that he undertook to rid the land of any remaining vestige of Canaanite and Assyrian idolatry and to centralize the temple cult. The "finding" of a law book (which some equate with the Book of Deuteronomy) provided the impetus for Josiah's reform, also called the Deuteronomic reform. Josiah died at Megiddo at the hands of the Egyptian Pharaoh Necho II in 609 B.C.E.

GLEANINGS

The Righteousness of Women

The story of Israelite slavery and subsequent freedom is the centerpiece of the Torah. Here Israelite identity is formed; from a tribe, to a band of slaves, to a people. Before the book of Exodus we have stories of heroes and heroines, who, though human, represent our more ancient mythological beginnings. With the story of Moses, the Torah becomes our history, whose climax is known: the giving of the law at Sinai. The story of Egypt is crucial not only because of its critique of slavery, but because of its positive and moralistic ending. Once bonded to Pharaoh, we are now bonded to God. Once servants to humans, we become servants to God.

There is no freedom from rules or rulership at Sinai. However, the locus of those rules has changed from human hands to the Mighty Arm of God. If we find spirituality in Exodus, it is a rule-based spirituality: Meet me at the Holy Mountain and bind yourself to Me as once you were bound to Pharaoh. You will be in relationship to God when you follow God's rules.

From a sociological perspective, one could analyze this grand theme of Exodus by using Carol Gilligan's model of the development of girls and boys. Boys, her studies suggest, develop a view of the world as a series of rules. Girls develop a view of the world as a series of relationships. The men of the Exodus story follow the rules, with the notable exception of the episode of the Golden Calf. The women work secretly against the rules, in favor of the value of human relationships. The men accept the rules at Sinai and get a reward: the priesthood, the land, tribal heads. But it is the women who keep the system running through their empathy and compassion.

Elyse Goldstein, *ReVisions: Seeing Torah Through a Feminist Lens*
(Woodstock, Vt.: Jewish Lights Publishing, 1999), 208

Honoring What Is Broken

Jewish texts abound with comments on aging.... Although deferential treatment toward the elderly originates with the commandment to honor one's parents, Jewish tradition broadens this to include *all* elderly. This reverence is articulated often in Jewish texts, most notably in Leviticus 19:32, "Rise before the gray headed...show deference to the old." And it is age, not status, that entitles the individual to respect. In Judaism, even what is "broken" is honored: The first set of tablets that Moses received from God and subsequently smashed was, according to *midrash*, placed in the Ark alongside the whole tablets. The tablets were holy and had not lost their holiness by being broken. And so the elderly, who may be ill or needy, are still whole and holy and deserve our attention and respect.

Susan Berrin, ed., *A Heart of Wisdom: Making the Jewish Journey from Midlife Through the Elder Years*
(Woodstock, Vt.: Jewish Lights Publishing, 1997), XXI

Remembering

Memory is the connections. Meaning comes from what something is connected to. Something unconnected, unassociated with, unrelated to anything is literally meaningless. Conversely something connected, associated, linked with many things is supercharged with meaning. And the farther back in time the connections go, the greater the meaning. By joining pieces of our lives together we create ourselves, free ourselves. It's all in the order and the sequence. For this reason, memory may be more in the way things are stored, rather than what is stored.

It is not accidental that the great feast of remembering our redemption is called simply: The order. The arrangement and interconnectedness of each of the parts preserves the message, the meaning. The story, for instance, ends with redemption, not with slavery, first come the questions, then the answers, because I was once a slave, I must know how it feels.

Lawrence Kushner, *The Book of Words: Talking Spiritual Life, Living Spiritual Talk*
(Woodstock, Vt.: Jewish Lights Publishing, 1995), 88–89

May You, at Long Last, Rest in Peace

Since even good lives are filled with toil and turmoil, we remember our beloved dead by saying, after we mention their names, *alav/aleha ha-shalom*, peace be upon him/her. This is a hope that dates back to the Bible: "R. Levi b. Hita said: One who leaves a funeral should not say to the dead, 'Go unto peace' but, 'Go in peace'... because God said to Abraham, 'You shall go to your fathers in peace' [Gen. 15:15]" (M.K. 29a). Particularly when someone has suffered protracted emotional adversity or physical pain, the release promised by the peace of death can almost be welcomed. As R. Meir taught: "When a righteous man departs from the world, three groups of angels warmly receive him with the greeting of *shalom*. The first says, 'Let him enter in peace,' the second says, 'Let him rest on his couch,' and the third says, 'Each one that walked in righteousness' [Isa. 57:2]" (Num. R. 11.7). But even those whose lives have not been particularly troubled hope for an ultimate peace. So we read about Judah ha-Nasi: "As Rabbi was dying, he raised his fingers toward heaven and prayed, 'Sovereign of the Universe, it is revealed and known to you that I have labored in the study of Torah with all ten of my fingers and that I did not seek the benefits of this world with even the littlest of them. May it be Your will, therefore, that there be peace in my final resting place.' A Heavenly Voice then proclaimed, 'He shall enter into peace; they shall rest on their beds' [Isaiah 57:2]" (Ket. 104a). To this day at funerals and memorial services we intone the *El malei rahamim* prayer, "God, full of compassion..." which in resounding conclusion appeals: May *Adonai* be his/her possession and may his/her repose be *shalom*."

Eugene B. Borowitz and Frances Weinman Schwartz, *The Jewish Moral Virtues*
(Philadelphia: Jewish Publication Society, 1999), 244

CHAPTER EIGHT

ח:א מִי כְּהֶחָכָם וּמִי יוֹדֵעַ פֵּשֶׁר דָּבָר חָכְמַת אָדָם תָּאִיר פָּנָיו וְעֹז פָּנָיו
יְשֻׁנֶּא:

8:1 Who is like the wise person? And who can discern a thing's inner meaning? Wisdom may enable a person to appear gracious even while rudeness is being disguised.

This is a difficult verse. Our translation of *pesher* as "inner meaning" follows Rashi's joining of *raz* (secret) and *pishrin* (meanings), possibly on the basis of Daniel 4:6. Kohelet uses two idioms related to *panim* (literally, "face"): *ta-ir panav* and *oz panav*. The first literally means "to make one's face shine" and idiomatically means "to appear gracious." The second literally means "to be strong of face." While there is no evidence of its use elsewhere, it may be related to *az panim* (as in Deuteronomy 28:50 and Daniel 8:23). If this is the case, then it has the meaning of "being rude" or "disrespectful." *Y'shuneh* (literally, "will be changed") has the sense of "disguise" in I Samuel 21:14, Psalm 34:1, and I Kings 14:2. Taking the verse as a whole, the message seems to be: wise is that person who can discern what is hidden behind appearances. A wise person can penetrate the disguise of another, even in the case of the cleverly rude person who appears to be gracious.

ח:ב אֲנִי פִּי־מֶלֶךְ שְׁמוֹר וְעַל דִּבְרַת שְׁבוּעַת אֱלֹהִים:

8:2 I say: Obey the order of the sovereign and that of an oath to God.

Our translation of *ani* (literally, "I") as "I say" follows Ibn Ezra, who takes the word to mean either *atzavecha* (I command you) or *azhirecha* (I warn you). Again, as might be expected, Rashi takes the sovereign to refer to God, the Sovereign of sovereigns. Ibn Ezra relates this verse to a previous verse that warned the wise person against the folly of lust. For him, this verse warns the wise person against the folly of disobeying a sovereign ruler, albeit a mortal one. Elsewhere in wisdom literature (Proverbs 19:12 and 20:2), the reader is warned against provoking the wrath of the sovereign. This is sound advice for any time and place where a ruler can exercise absolute and unchecked power.

ח:ג אַל־תִּבָּהֵל מִפָּנָיו תֵּלֵךְ אַל־תַּעֲמֹד בְּדָבָר רָע כִּי כָּל־אֲשֶׁר יַחְפֹּץ יַעֲשֶׂה:

8:3 DON'T HASTEN TO LEAVE THE SOVEREIGN'S PRESENCE. BUT DON'T STAND AROUND WHERE THERE IS SOMETHING BAD HAPPENING, FOR A SOVEREIGN HAS AUTHORITY.

While this is a difficult verse to translate precisely, Kohelet is telling the reader to beware of power—not to take chances with it. Some scholars (including Koehler and Baumgartner, p. 111) suggest adding the first two words of this verse (*al tibaheil*, "don't hasten") to the last clause of the previous verse. That verse would then conclude, "Don't hasten to take an oath to God." Thus, the first clause of this verse would read, "Leave the sovereign's presence; don't stand around where there is something bad happening." Such a change would make the text read more smoothly. It would join the verb *tibaheil* to an act of speech in a similar manner to the way Kohelet uses the verb in 5:1 (where we have translated it as "rush") or as an act of thought in 7:9 (where we have translated it as "be quick"). Rashi, of course, accepts the text as it stands and, relating the verse to God, the Divine Ruler, has Kohelet tell the reader not to be hasty to flee from the Divine Presence because there is no place where that Presence is lacking. Although Ibn Ezra takes the verse to refer to the power of a mortal ruler, he takes it as sound advice in dealing with such power.

ח:ד בַּאֲשֶׁר דְּבַר־מֶלֶךְ שִׁלְטוֹן וּמִי יֹאמַר־לוֹ מַה־תַּעֲשֶׂה:

8:4 SINCE THE WORLD OF A SOVEREIGN IS POWER, WHO CAN SAY TO THE SOVEREIGN, WHAT ARE YOU DOING?

We have translated the pronoun "him" as "sovereign" in order to avoid gender specificity. *Shilton* (dominion, power) suggests that force, not virtue, is the basis of the power behind the sovereign's word. Why will no one say, "What are you doing?" For Rashi, the sovereign is God, the Divine Sovereign, and no one may question God's actions. For Ibn Ezra, the sovereign is a mortal ruler, but nobody will challenge a mortal king or queen because they are afraid to do so.

ח:ה שׁוֹמֵר מִצְוָה לֹא יֵדַע דָּבָר רָע וְעֵת וּמִשְׁפָּט יֵדַע לֵב חָכָם:

8:5 ONE WHO KEEPS THE COMMANDMENT WILL NOT KNOW TROUBLE, FOR A WISE MIND KNOWS THERE IS A TIME FOR JUDGMENT.

Although the Hebrew text is relatively simple, this verse is difficult to understand, because the reader cannot tell from the context who issued the *mitzvah* (commandment) in the first clause and who determines the *eit u'mishpat* (the time for judgment) in the second clause. Perhaps it is a mortal ruler. Perhaps it is God. If it is God, as Rashi suggests, then it is God who issued the commandment. Rashi understands *eit* as "set time" and translates *mishpat* (judgment) with the Old French *justicia* (justice). If it is a mortal ruler, then *mitzvah* is merely an "order," but then the reader is left to puzzle out what is meant by *eit u'mishpat* in this verse and the verse that follows. One does not look for ultimate justice from mortal kings and queens. *Mishpat* could mean "custom," "manner of life," or even "style" (according to Koehler and Baumgartner). So *eit u'mishpat* could mean "time and manner." Thus, the wise mind would know that there is a time and a style for everything. There is another possible resolution to the challenge implicit in interpreting this verse. Perhaps Kohelet is simply quoting a proverb about God— or something he learned while much younger—which he will refute in verses 7–9, which follow. This is suggested by the next verse.

ח:ו כִּי לְכָל־חֵפֶץ יֵשׁ עֵת וּמִשְׁפָּט כִּי־רָעַת הָאָדָם רַבָּה עָלָיו:

8:6 EVERYTHING HAS ITS TIME FOR JUDGMENT BECAUSE HUMAN EVIL HAS GROWN SO GREAT.

Comparing this verse to verses in the previous chapter (7:15–18), there is the feeling that Kohelet is not much troubled by the evil in this world. Yet this verse, which seems to invoke God's judgment, would be the kind of verse that conventional religion would trumpet. Rashi understands the verse to mean that when wickedness increases, so does its punishment. Ibn Ezra takes the first clause to mean that a wise person does not contend with one upon whom fortune smiles. He takes the second clause to mean that it is a great evil for such wise persons not to know when fortune will smile upon them.

ח:ז כִּי־אֵינֶנּוּ יֹדֵעַ מַה־שֶּׁיִּהְיֶה כִּי כַּאֲשֶׁר יִהְיֶה מִי יַגִּיד לוֹ:

8:7 ONE DOES NOT KNOW WHAT WILL BE, AND IF IT WERE TO BE, WHO WOULD TELL HIM [OR HER]?

This verse may be taken as a kind of refutation of the two prior verses, a new realization on Kohelet's behalf. Perhaps there is a time for judgment, but who knows where or when? And if one does not know, what difference can judgment make? Rashi, who accepts the notion of divine judgment, bemoans the wicked who, having transgressed, are not aware that they will receive an appropriate punishment. If this is so, even Rashi's case suggests that an unknown punishment has no effect on preventing the commission of evil acts. Ibn Ezra notes that even if people know in general that they will be punished for their evil acts, they do not know the particularities of their punishment.

ח:ח אֵין אָדָם שַׁלִּיט בָּרוּחַ לִכְלוֹא אֶת־הָרוּחַ וְאֵין שִׁלְטוֹן בְּיוֹם הַמָּוֶת וְאֵין מִשְׁלַחַת בַּמִּלְחָמָה וְלֹא־יְמַלֵּט רֶשַׁע אֶת־בְּעָלָיו:

8:8 NO ONE HAS POWER OVER THE WIND, TO HOLD BACK THE WIND. NO ONE HAS POWER OVER THE DAY OF DEATH, AND THERE IS NO DEFERMENT [OF IT] IN WAR. WEALTH WILL NOT SAVE THOSE WHO HAVE IT.

Although the *Targum*, Rashi, and Ibn Ezra take *ruach* to mean "the human spirit" or "soul," defining *ruach* as "wind" makes sense here. However, these commentators are attempting to make the connection between "death" and the "soul." Kohelet is saying that there are some things in nature over which we have no control. We can't control the blowing of the wind, nor can we confine it. We can't control the fact that every mortal will die; that is what it means to be human. Kohelet also says that there are some things that may start out under human control, but that control will eventually be lost. When war breaks out, it is hard to get a deferment even when it seems appropriate. These ideas are evidenced most clearly in the Mishnah (*Sotah* 8) that is a commentary on Deuteronomy 20:2–9, which lists the various categories of men who are entitled to deferments during a war: the builder of a new house, a new husband, and one who is a coward. In the Mishnah we read that these deferments are only relevant to "a voluntary war, but a war fought for a religious purpose, all go out, even the bridegroom from his chamber and the bride from hers." Moreover, when war breaks out, anyone can get killed: rich or poor, good or evil. The last clause of the verse, *v'lo y'maleit resha et b'alav*, can be translated as "wickedness will not save the wicked." Such a translation is problematic. *B'alav* usually means "its [or his] owners." If we are to accept the Masoretic text, we have to take *resha* (wickedness) as the subject of *y'maleit* (will save) and then have to assume that *b'alav* were the owners of "wickedness" and hence translated as "wicked." However, Ibn Ezra was troubled by the verse and suggested an odd translation for *resha* (wickedness) that is related to money, since most evil is done for money. Some scholars recommend an easier way out of the difficulty. If we reverse the letters of *resha*, assuming an error in scribal transmission, we get the word *osher* (wealth). *Osher* works with "owners" and makes sense of the clause "wealth will not save its owners."

ח:ט אֶת־כָּל־זֶה רָאִיתִי וְנָתוֹן אֶת־לִבִּי לְכָל־מַעֲשֶׂה אֲשֶׁר נַעֲשָׂה תַּחַת הַשֶּׁמֶשׁ עֵת אֲשֶׁר שָׁלַט הָאָדָם בְּאָדָם לְרַע לוֹ:

8:9 ALL OF THIS DID I SEE WHEN I PAID ATTENTION TO EVERYTHING DONE BENEATH THE SUN, WHENEVER ONE PERSON HAD THE POWER OVER ANOTHER TO DO THAT PERSON HARM.

Making a reference to the previous verse in his comment on this verse, Ibn Ezra warns the person who would be wise about the unchecked power of a sovereign ruler. Such power allows for every manner of evil.

82

ח:י וּבְכֵן רָאִיתִי רְשָׁעִים קְבֻרִים וָבָאוּ וּמִמְּקוֹם קָדוֹשׁ יְהַלֵּכוּ וְיִשְׁתַּכְּחוּ בָעִיר אֲשֶׁר כֵּן־עָשׂוּ גַּם־זֶה הָבֶל:

8:10 THIS TOO DID I SEE: THE WICKED BROUGHT TO
BURIAL, AND THEY CAME AND WOULD GO FROM THE
HOLY PLACE, AND THEY WOULD BE FORGOTTEN IN
THE CITY WHERE THUS THEY HAD ACTED—BUT THIS
TOO IS USELESS.

This is a difficult verse. In the first clause, *vava-u* (and they came) does not quite
fit into the context. On the basis of various versions of the text, the editor of
Biblia Hebraica recommends that this word *(vava-u)* should be emended, as should
the word that precedes it. Then the words are joined together to form *k'varim
muva-im* (brought to burial) from *k'vurim vava-u* (buried and they came). It should be
noted that the final *m* would come from the *m* (from) of the next word. There is also
a question about the meaning of the phrase *m'kom kadosh* (holy place). From
the commentary of the *Targum,* one would think that it is *atar kadish d'tzadikaya
sharyan taman* "the place where the righteous rest" and from which the wicked are
removed *vaazalu l'itokda big'hinam* (to go and burn in *Geihinom*). Thus, it would
mean a cemetery. For Rashi, it is "the House of God," the Temple. There is also a
question about *v'yishtak'chu* (they would be forgotten). Quoting a variant reading of
the Talmud, (Babylonian Talmud, *Gittin* 56b), Rashi suggests a different reading:
vishatabchu (and they praise themselves). Ibn Ezra presents two commentaries to
the verse that he thinks are mistaken: Some understand *r'shaim k'vurim* to mean
"the wicked are protected [buried] in their castles"; *vava-u . . . y'haleichu*, "they come
and go," that is, they come and do whatever they want (in the holy place);
v'yishtak'chu (from the Aramaic root *sh'chiach*, "to find"), "they are found" (in the
city). Others interpret *vava-u* (and they come) as "they disappear" (as in the phrase
uva hashemesh, "the sun sets," that is, disappears). Ibn Ezra offers his own
interpretation as he links this verse to the previous one. There are wicked people
who harmed others because they had the power to do so. Yet they die without
suffering and are brought to the grave without pain (an allusion to Psalm 73:4).
They come to the other world (the holy place), and their children arrive and take
their place and their memory is preserved. The phrase *mimkom kadosh y'haleichu*
refers to those righteous persons, the *k'doshim* (the saints) who die without progeny
and are forgotten in the city even though they are *asher kein asu* (they acted rightly).
Ibn Ezra's interpretation of *kein* as "rightly" follows its usage in Numbers 27:7.
Kohelet, Ibn Ezra continues, is troubled that the memory of the righteous who died
without children is cut off and all the good done by them is forgotten, while the
wicked lived and died in prosperity and left children to take their place. It should
be noted that nowhere in this verse is there any mention of the "righteous."
Therefore, any contrast between the wicked and the righteous wherever it may
take place has been read into the verse by the *Targum* and the commentators.
Kohelet's message may be quite simple: the wicked get away with it, even in death.

When they die, they are buried. Their bodies are brought to and from a holy place for the funeral. However, their evil acts are forgotten even in the very city where they occurred.

ח:יא אֲשֶׁר אֵין־נַעֲשָׂה פִתְגָם מַעֲשֵׂה הָרָעָה מְהֵרָה עַל־כֵּן מָלֵא לֵב בְּנֵי־הָאָדָם בָּהֶם לַעֲשׂוֹת רָע:

8:11 BECAUSE THE VERDICT UPON AN EVIL ACT IS NOT CARRIED OUT SWIFTLY, PEOPLE ARE ENCOURAGED TO DO EVIL.

Kohelet points out a pragmatic problem that emerges from what appears to be ethical agnosticism. If it is true, as the last verse suggested, that the quality of a person's death does not indicate anything about the quality of that person's life, and if it is true that there is no immediate correlation between virtue and its reward and vice and its punishment, then those truths have a negative impact on society. If it is the fear of punishment that keeps some from doing wrong, then any delay in the application of that punishment may remove that fear, as Ibn Ezra noted. Such people would have no disincentive from doing wrong. As might be imagined, Rashi relates the verse to the acts of the Divine Judge, while Ibn Ezra relates it to the acts of a human judge.

ח:יב אֲשֶׁר חֹטֶא עֹשֶׂה רָע מְאַת וּמַאֲרִיךְ לוֹ כִּי גַם־יוֹדֵעַ אָנִי אֲשֶׁר יִהְיֶה־טּוֹב לְיִרְאֵי הָאֱלֹהִים אֲשֶׁר יִירְאוּ מִלְּפָנָיו:

8:12 FOR A SINNER MAY DO EVIL ONE HUNDRED TIMES, YET GOD WILL BE PATIENT. I INDEED KNOW THAT IT WILL BE WELL WITH THOSE WHO ARE GOD-FEARING, BECAUSE THEY REVERE GOD.

The *Targum*, Rashi, and Ibn Ezra take *maarich* (be patient) as a reference to God. The *Targum* explains why God is patient: *b'gin d'yituv,* "that the sinner may repent." Rashi adds to the number of evil acts performed, not merely "one hundred" but "thousands" and even "tens of thousands." Even so, Rashi adds, one knows that the righteous will be rewarded and the wicked will be requited. It seems that this verse and the one that follows contradict the one that precedes this verse. Perhaps it is a result of Kohelet's newfound piety. Perhaps it is something that he learned in later life. Here he rejects the opinion of his youth. Maybe he is quoting an opinion that is held by members of his community, which he is rejecting. Or maybe he is making an ironic statement: if any delay in the punishment of evil encourages evildoers, then divine delay does the same!

ח:יג וְטוֹב לֹא־יִהְיֶה לָרָשָׁע וְלֹא־יַאֲרִיךְ יָמִים כַּצֵּל אֲשֶׁר אֵינֶנּוּ יָרֵא מִלִּפְנֵי אֱלֹהִים:

8:13 It will not be well for the wicked, because they do not fear God. They, like a shadow, will not endure long.

This is another statement that seems to reflect Kohelet's piety. According to Ibn Ezra, although Kohelet experienced what was described in the prior verse—just as other intelligent people have done so—Kohelet has come to the conclusion expressed in this verse, just as he knows others have done so. For Ibn Ezra and Kohelet, the key is reverence for God. Only a belief in reward and punishment in the next world can justify this verse. Yet, Kohelet expressed doubt in 3:21 about the individual's ability to transcend death. Thus, we see once again how Kohelet contradicts what he has written. Perhaps this verse is a gloss that was added by a later editor to make the text more religiously acceptable and consistent with the theology of Rabbinic Judaism. Or perhaps what this verse represents is a more mature approach to life, one that emerges at the end of Kohelet's life experience. By saying one thing in one verse and then contradicting what appears to be his own statement, it may be that Kohelet is really disputing the commonly held wisdom that he stated previously.

ח:יד יֶשׁ־הֶבֶל אֲשֶׁר נַעֲשָׂה עַל־הָאָרֶץ אֲשֶׁר יֵשׁ צַדִּיקִים אֲשֶׁר מַגִּיעַ אֲלֵהֶם כְּמַעֲשֵׂה הָרְשָׁעִים וְיֵשׁ רְשָׁעִים שֶׁמַּגִּיעַ אֲלֵהֶם כְּמַעֲשֵׂה הַצַּדִּיקִים אָמַרְתִּי שֶׁגַּם־זֶה הָבֶל:

8:14 What happens on earth is useless. Innocent people get what guilty people deserve, and guilty people get what innocent people deserve. I said that this too is useless.

That the wicked are rewarded and the righteous are punished seems to undermine what Kohelet just wrote in 8:13. The relationship between virtue and its reward, and vice and its punishment, remains a problem for theodicy. Rashi explains the first use of the word *hevel* in this verse to mean ''startles'' or ''confuses'' people.

ח:טו וְשִׁבַּחְתִּי אֲנִי אֶת־הַשִּׂמְחָה אֲשֶׁר אֵין־טוֹב לָאָדָם תַּחַת הַשֶּׁמֶשׁ כִּי אִם־לֶאֱכוֹל וְלִשְׁתּוֹת וְלִשְׂמוֹחַ וְהוּא יִלְוֶנּוּ בַעֲמָלוֹ יְמֵי חַיָּיו אֲשֶׁר־נָתַן־לוֹ הָאֱלֹהִים תַּחַת הַשָּׁמֶשׁ:

8:15 SO I PRAISED JOY, FOR THERE IS NOTHING BETTER FOR A PERSON BENEATH THE SUN THAN TO EAT AND DRINK AND BE JOYFUL. IN ALL THAT YOU DO, LET IT BE YOUR COMPANION, IN ALL THE DAYS OF LIFE THAT GOD HAS GIVEN YOU BENEATH THE SUN.

Kohelet returns to a theme that he mentioned in 5:17. If there is neither justice in this world, nor an accounting for one's deeds in the next world, then the best that one can do is enjoy the world in which one lives. Thus, there is some compensation for one's trials and tribulations. In a comment that comes as no surprise, Rashi takes "eat and drink and be joyful" to refer to the study of Torah.

ח:טז כַּאֲשֶׁר נָתַתִּי אֶת־לִבִּי לָדַעַת חָכְמָה וְלִרְאוֹת אֶת־הָעִנְיָן אֲשֶׁר נַעֲשָׂה עַל־הָאָרֶץ כִּי גַם בַּיּוֹם וּבַלַּיְלָה שֵׁנָה בְּעֵינָיו אֵינֶנּוּ רֹאֶה:

8:16 WHEN I SET MY MIND TO ACQUIRE WISDOM AND TO SEE EVERYTHING THAT TAKES PLACE ON EARTH, MY EYES DID NOT EVEN SEE SLEEP, NIGHT OR DAY.

Rashi takes the first word, *kaasher* (when), to mean "for example." Ibn Ezra takes it to mean "no sooner," that is, "no sooner had I taken on joy" than I began to pursue "wisdom." The *Targum*, as expected, understands wisdom as *chuchmat Oraita*, "the wisdom of Torah."

ח:יז וְרָאִיתִי אֶת־כָּל־מַעֲשֵׂה הָאֱלֹהִים כִּי לֹא יוּכַל הָאָדָם לִמְצוֹא אֶת־הַמַּעֲשֶׂה אֲשֶׁר נַעֲשָׂה תַחַת־הַשֶּׁמֶשׁ בְּשֶׁל אֲשֶׁר יַעֲמֹל הָאָדָם לְבַקֵּשׁ וְלֹא יִמְצָא וְגַם אִם־יֹאמַר הֶחָכָם לָדַעַת לֹא יוּכַל לִמְצֹא:

8:17 LOOKING AT ALL THE WORK OF GOD, I SAW THAT NO HUMAN CAN DISCOVER WHAT IS DONE BENEATH THE SUN. NO MATTER HOW HARD YOU TRY TO SEEK IT OUT, YOU WON'T FIND IT. EVEN IF A WISE PERSON WOULD THINK THAT ONE COULD KNOW IT, IT IS NOT POSSIBLE TO DISCOVER IT.

You cannot guess, but Kohelet knows. Does this make him wiser than the Sages? The *Targum* explains why humans lack such human knowledge: *arum d'chilah hu v'leit leih r'shu leenash l'ashkacha,* "because it is awesome and humans lack permission to find it. . . ." For Rashi, it is the sight of the wicked succeeding and the righteous failing that causes people to despair of knowing how reward and punishment work. Ibn Ezra notes that Job was concerned with the same question.

Masoretic Text

Jewish scribes working from 500 to 1000 C.E. were known as the Masoretes. They meticulously copied the Scriptures and preserved them. The work of the Masoretes resulted in the Masoretic text of the Bible, the Hebrew text that is the standard today. They also set the musical notes for reading known in Yiddish as *trope* and in Hebrew as *taamei hamikra.*

Biblia Hebraica

Biblia Hebraica is a "critical edition" of the Bible that scholars employ as a tool to understand and interpret the biblical text. It comprises readings of the text as contained in variant editions and manuscripts with suggestions for emendation (in order to understand confusing texts) based on these editions. It was prepared by Rudolph Kittel early in the twentieth century. A revised edition is scheduled for publication in the early twenty-first century.

Divine Punishment/Divine Judge

Kohelet is a book of wisdom. Thus, what the author offers the reader is gleaned from his experience in life. As he reports, he often sees sinners go unpunished. Following the biblical period, the Rabbis introduced the notion of the next world, which seems to balance the injustice that they perceived taking place in this world. In other words, if we see sinners who go unpunished, we should not worry, because God will punish them in the next world. However, the Torah has the notion of *kareit,* literally "cutting off." This is often interpreted as the means through which God punishes those who do evil: their lives are shorter than they should be. This idea also goes against the experience of many in this world.

GLEANINGS

Norms in Reform Judaism

Ours is the task—by no means an easy one—of forging a Reform Judaism that will correct the excessive individualism upon which so much Reform thought and teaching have concentrated. [Samuel] Holdheim and others, informed by a Kantian vision of autonomy, permitted their ties to Jewish norms to erode—in part—because the writings of [Immanuel] Kant on autonomy and the nature of the self appeared to them as true and self-sufficient. Their trust in the promise of reason was absolute. Ours is a different age. Their certitudes are no longer ours, and we seek a communitarian expression of freedom and relationship distinct from the teachings they expounded. We will look to the norms of our tradition to aid us in that quest, and however halting and tentative our efforts, we Reform Jews, like all Jews past and present, will search for the holiness that is ours as heirs to the Covenantal patrimony that is our heritage.

Over seven decades ago, Franz Rosenzweig, in his inaugural address at the Frankfurt Lehrhaus, invited his students to see that their learning could constitute a "kind of remembrance, an inner remembering, a turning from externals to that which is within, a turning that, believe me, will and must become for you a returning home." And, in concluding, he offered them the following directive. He said, "Turn into yourself, return home to your innermost self and to your innermost life" ["On Jewish Learning," in Nahum N. Glatzer, *Franz Rosenzweig: His Life and Thought* (New York: Schocken, 1972), 234]. May these words and the spirit that informs them guide and crown our own approach and efforts as we seek to educate ourselves and our people. For they beckon us to teach and live in integrity as Jews, mindful of the seriousness of the task to which we as Jews have been called.

David Ellenson, "Autonomy and Norms in Reform Judaism," in *CCAR Journal: A Reform Jewish Quarterly* (spring 1999): 27–28

The Sense of Mitzvah

In reality, what we are proposing for most Reform Jews is a *change in lifestyle*. It may seem an impossible task. However, as we look around we see a remarkable thing happening. People are changing their lifestyles. We are paying attention to our bodies. We are changing our diets. We are losing weight. We are joining health clubs. We jog; we exercise; we play tennis and racquetball; we swim and do aerobics. We do it because it makes us feel better. We do it because it makes us look better. We do it because we want to live longer. Doctors tell us what to do. Our friends encourage us by their admiring comments. Television commercials, news programs, newspaper columns tells us we are part of a trend, and, by God, it works, it makes a difference in the way we look and the way we feel. It is not always easy to get up early to exercise, but we do it religiously and we feel badly when we have to skip a day. The rich desserts, the fatty foods, the extra sprinkle of salt, the spoonful of sugar, and the caffeine in the coffee remain temptations. Sometimes we cheat a little but we go back and try again. But we know that *I* won't lose weight if *you* diet. And that *my* blood pressure won't improve if *you* exercise. It only works if we do it ourselves. But it is so much easier if we do it together.

I wish to suggest an outrageous image. We are all part of the health club. It is called the Jewish People. Our ancestors willed us a lifelong membership called the Covenant. There is a program of exercise and diet for creating Jewish spiritual health. It is called Torah and mitzvot. As any good program, it is challenging but not too difficult. If we follow it faithfully, the benefits are great. If we follow the program, we will get in shape.

Peter S. Knobel, "Personal Autonomy and the Sense of Mitzvah,"
Yearbook of the Central Conference of American Rabbis 96 (1986): 43

Balance

This is life's lesson I am currently learning: how to balance engaging with life while remaining in the moment.

A piece of Chasidic wisdom from the 18th century says: "Just as the hand, held before the eye, can hide the tallest mountain, so the routine of everyday life can keep us from seeing the vast radiance and the secret wonders that fill the world."

Sometimes I find it quite challenging to remove the hand from in front of my eye. As I stand in front of a microwave gobbling down reheated leftovers, I'm not really tasting or savoring the food passing over my tongue. While, from a taste standpoint, that may be a good thing that's for another discussion! In our day and age of quick food, experts from nutritionists to family therapists bemoan the loss of people eating and socializing together. For me, there's also a spiritual aspect that is lost as I simply shovel food down. I know that I'm not respecting my body or taking the time to be thankful for the bounty bestowed upon me. In contrast, I have found how fulfilling a meal is for me when I take the time to eat slowly, especially in the company of close friends and/or family. . . .

But as we've created technologies to save us time, for many of us, our lives have gotten busier, more scheduled. It's unrealistic for me to suggest that any one of us can ignore our responsibilities and simply head to the beach or the mountains. However, each of us takes on additional responsibilities that we could probably graciously turn down. Some years ago a mentor told me to make sure that I didn't take on too many responsibilities so I wouldn't burn out. I value that teaching, since I'm hoping to be interacting and engaged with others for many years to come.

To guard against burnout, we need to make sure that we carve out some time for us. As Golda Meir said, "I must govern the clock, not be governed by it." So must we govern our lives, which for me means participating in activities that feed my soul so that I can perform the necessary parts of life that may not be as fun or engaging.

But in our fast-paced, and sometimes very scripted culture, what does it mean to live life? The Jerusalem Talmud [K1:7] interprets life as defined by how we educate our children. It instructs parents to "teach their children a profession and the art of swimming." It goes on to say that if the parent is derelict in this duty, children are obligated to pursue these skills themselves.

The idea of being able to take responsibility for my own life education was wonderfully liberating. What this tractate says to me is that if we as adults feel we haven't received the necessary skills to live our lives from our upbringing, it is incumbent upon us to develop these skills as we realize we need them. Most of us did not grow up being taught how beautiful it is for lovers, be they two men or two women, to kiss passionately. Most of us did not grow up recognizing that genitalia don't necessarily determine gender. Growing up I was fortunate that my parents didn't have specific expectations of me other than to do my best. I remember my mother telling me that it would be fine if I wanted to be a gas station attendant as long as I was the best gas station attendant I could be. If I pursued my dreams with all the energy and intellect that I had; that if whatever I did, I did to the best of my ability, and was happy, then she would be proud of me. That is such a powerful message: live life to the best of your ability and you're living life to its fullest.

Howard Steiermann (Rosh HaShanah sermon, Congregation Sha'ar Zahav,
San Francisco, Calif., 2000), 1–3

CHAPTER NINE

ט:א כִּי אֶת־כָּל־זֶה נָתַתִּי אֶל־לִבִּי וְלָבוּר אֶת־כָּל־זֶה אֲשֶׁר הַצַּדִּיקִים
וְהַחֲכָמִים וַעֲבָדֵיהֶם בְּיַד הָאֱלֹהִים גַּם־אַהֲבָה גַּם־שִׂנְאָה אֵין יוֹדֵעַ
הָאָדָם הַכֹּל לִפְנֵיהֶם:

9:1 ALL THIS HAVE I REFLECTED ON AND IT BECAME CLEAR
TO ME THAT EVEN ALL THE DEEDS OF THE RIGHTEOUS
AND THE WISE ARE IN GOD'S HANDS. WHETHER LOVE OR
WHETHER HATE, NONE KNOW WHAT LIES BEFORE THEM.

This is a difficult verse. *V'avadeihem* is taken by the *Targum* and Rashi as "and their
servants," that is, their students. It is taken by Ibn Ezra—and by most modern
scholars—as "their deeds." The *Targum,* Rashi, and Ibn Ezra differ as to what or who
is the source of the "love" and "hate" mentioned in this verse. According to the
Targum, b'mazalaya itg'zar refers "to the constellations." According to Rashi, God is
the source. And for Ibn Ezra, humans are the source of love and hate. For the *Targum,*
not even a prophet can foretell the impact of love or hate. For Rashi, individuals do
not know whether or not they are beloved of God. For Ibn Ezra, individuals do not
know whether or not they will experience love or hate. The simple meaning of the
verse is that whether in the hands of God or of fate, the individual has little ability to
influence outcomes, for even the wise and the virtuous cannot be sure of God's love,
to say nothing of its effect on the constellations!

ט:ב הַכֹּל כַּאֲשֶׁר לַכֹּל מִקְרֶה אֶחָד לַצַּדִּיק וְלָרָשָׁע לַטּוֹב וְלַטָּהוֹר
וְלַטָּמֵא וְלַזֹּבֵחַ וְלַאֲשֶׁר אֵינֶנּוּ זֹבֵחַ כַּטּוֹב כַּחֹטֶא הַנִּשְׁבָּע כַּאֲשֶׁר
שְׁבוּעָה יָרֵא:

9:2 THE SAME THING HAPPENS TO EVERYONE. ONE FATE
FOR THE INNOCENT AND THE GUILTY, FOR THE GOOD
AND THE PURE AND FOR THE IMPURE, FOR THE ONE
WHO BRINGS SACRIFICES AND FOR THE ONE WHO DOES
NOT. THE SAME THING HAPPENS TO THE ONE WHO IS
GOOD AND TO THE ONE WHO IS A SINNER, TO THE ONE
WHO TAKES AN OATH AND TO THE ONE WHO IS AFRAID
[TO DO SO].

Kohelet clearly means more than the obvious meaning of the verse: all human beings
die. He means that what happens to people is not a function of their virtue or their

91

vice or of their ritual compliance or their lack of it. Like the Book of Job, this book presents a challenge to the prophetic notion that good is rewarded and evil is punished. This verse and others scattered throughout the Book of *Kohelet* challenge a basic assumption of biblical religion. Since, as we have seen, the author doubts the possibility of an individual's ability to somehow transcend physical death—the "system saver" introduced by Rabbinic Judaism—it is not available to Kohelet the writer or to those readers who agree with him. Since the world-to-come is an acceptable notion for Rashi, and since he maintains that there are distinctions in that world between those who are good and those who have sinned, Rashi has no compunctions about giving examples in this world where there are no distinctions made. Thus, for example, Moses, who was "good," and Aaron, who was "pure," did not enter the Land of Israel, just like the spies, who were "impure." As in the previous verse, the author of the *Targum* explains the source of fate as *kola b'mazalaya talya,* "everything depends on the constellations."

ט:ג זֶה רָע בְּכֹל אֲשֶׁר־נַעֲשָׂה תַּחַת הַשֶּׁמֶשׁ כִּי־מִקְרֶה אֶחָד לַכֹּל וְגַם לֵב בְּנֵי־הָאָדָם מָלֵא־רָע וְהוֹלֵלוֹת בִּלְבָבָם בְּחַיֵּיהֶם וְאַחֲרָיו אֶל־הַמֵּתִים:

9:3 THAT THERE IS A COMMON FATE IS THE CAUSE OF EVIL IN ALL THAT IS DONE BENEATH THE SUN. SO TOO THE HUMAN HEART IS FILLED WITH EVIL. THERE IS MADNESS WHILE PEOPLE ARE LIVING, AND AFTERWARDS, WITH THE DEAD.

The folly in their lives will accompany them to their graves. If one thinks that reward is the only incentive for virtue and punishment the only disincentive, then one must conclude that the lack of reward and punishment must move the individual to vice and the common fate of death must fill the mind with evil. In this verse, Kohelet affirms his earlier view (8:11) that the delay of justice motivates the doing of evil. Rashi claims that people's minds are "filled with evil" if they think that it is mere chance that governs human affairs. The end of such a person will be with "the dead," for they will descend into *Geihinom.*

ט:ד כִּי־מִי אֲשֶׁר יְבֻחַר יְחֻבַּר אֶל כָּל־הַחַיִּים יֵשׁ בִּטָּחוֹן כִּי־לְכֶלֶב חַי הוּא טוֹב מִן־הָאַרְיֵה הַמֵּת:

9:4 HOWEVER, ONE LINKED TO LIFE HAS ASSURANCE, FOR A LIVE DOG IS BETTER THAN A DEAD LION.

The translation of the word *bitachon* (assurance) is the focus of the problem in translating and interpreting this verse. The word occurs three times in the Bible (II Kings 18:19; Isaiah 36:4; and this verse). In the first two instances, which report the same event, a question asked of Hezekiah by the king of Babylon, the word might well be translated as "assurance" as in "What assurance do you have?" Both the *Targum* and Rashi take the word to mean "hope." Since the former understands "life" to refer to *pitgamei oraita* (words of Torah), it translates *bitachon* as *sevar* (hope) and explains "hope" as *ul'miknei chaya alma d'atei,* "to acquire life in the world-to-come." The latter takes *bitachon* to mean "hope" because the wicked may repent before they die. Even so, one can argue that *bitachon* does mean "assurance": the assurance that life itself gives. A lion can terrify, but a dead lion cannot do so. Whatever life is, it is better than death. Since death overtakes everyone, the only virtue in life is life itself. This seems to contradict what Kohelet has said in previous statements. Scholars suggest that either Kohelet is creating a straw argument or a narrator is repeating Kohelet's words and then refuting them. Perhaps these are both Kohelet's ideas. In his older years, Kohelet is reviewing what he wrote down early on and now refutes it.

ט:ה כִּי הַחַיִּים יוֹדְעִים שֶׁיָּמֻתוּ וְהַמֵּתִים אֵינָם יוֹדְעִים מְאוּמָה
וְאֵין־עוֹד לָהֶם שָׂכָר כִּי נִשְׁכַּח זִכְרָם:

9:5 THOSE WHO ARE ALIVE KNOW THAT THEY WILL DIE.
THOSE WHO ARE DEAD KNOW NOTHING. THEY HAVE
NO FURTHER REWARD. THEIR MEMORY IS FORGOTTEN.

Dead is dead. Since the *Targum* and Rashi believe that true reward and punishment occur after death in the world-to-come, they both understand the first clause as a call to repentance. According to Ibn Ezra, even fools know while they are alive that they will die. However, even wise people will know nothing when they are dead. Therefore, the wise have nothing for which to hope. When they are dead, their fame and all memory of them will be lost. Kohelet denies the biblical concept of immortality by stating that there is no memory of the dead at all, not even by those who remain alive.

ט:ו גַּם אַהֲבָתָם גַּם־שִׂנְאָתָם גַּם־קִנְאָתָם כְּבָר אָבָדָה וְחֵלֶק אֵין־לָהֶם
עוֹד לְעוֹלָם בְּכֹל אֲשֶׁר־נַעֲשָׂה תַּחַת הַשָּׁמֶשׁ:

9:6 WHAT THEY LOVED, WHAT THEY HATED, AND WHAT
THEY WERE JEALOUS OF WILL ALL BE GONE. NEVER
AGAIN WILL THEY HAVE A SHARE IN ANYTHING DONE
BENEATH THE SUN.

Although the *Targum* and Rashi soften the impact of the verse by referring it exclusively to the wicked, the literal meaning of the verse carries a message flush with melancholy. Everything goes, even love and hate. After one dies, the individual no longer participates in activities. Again, this is a rejection of the biblical notion of the afterlife. For Kohelet, it seems that there can be no afterlife, not even through one's descendants.

ט:ז לֵךְ אֱכֹל בְּשִׂמְחָה לַחְמֶךָ וּשֲׁתֵה בְלֶב־טוֹב יֵינֶךָ כִּי כְבָר רָצָה הָאֱלֹהִים אֶת־מַעֲשֶׂיךָ:

9:7 Go, eat your bread with joy and with an easy mind. Drink your wine, for God has already approved what you have done.

If this life is all that counts and if death makes no distinctions between virtue and vice, nor between wealth and poverty, then you should live as well as you can. If you have accumulated wealth, then you should enjoy it. Moreover, it seems that the very possession of wealth argues for divine favor. As might be expected, the *Targum* and Rashi refer this verse to the righteous. Note that this verse and the two that follow it are cast in biblical poetic form, that is, with beats if not with rhyme.

ט:ח בְּכָל־עֵת יִהְיוּ בְגָדֶיךָ לְבָנִים וְשֶׁמֶן עַל־רֹאשְׁךָ אַל־יֶחְסָר:

9:8 Let your garments always be white, and let your head never lack for fragrant oil.

Although the *Targum* and Rashi take the first clause as a metaphor for the doing of good deeds and the second clause as a metaphor for the possession of a good name (that is, reputation), the literal sense of the verse is clear. It is a continuation of the idea that was initiated in the preceding verse, "if you've got it, flaunt it." The possession of white garments and the use of perfume reflect wealth and privilege.

ט:ט רְאֵה חַיִּים עִם־אִשָּׁה אֲשֶׁר־אָהַבְתָּ כָּל־יְמֵי חַיֵּי הֶבְלֶךָ אֲשֶׁר נָתַן־לְךָ תַּחַת הַשֶּׁמֶשׁ כֹּל יְמֵי הֶבְלֶךָ כִּי הוּא חֶלְקְךָ בַּחַיִּים וּבַעֲמָלְךָ אֲשֶׁר־אַתָּה עָמֵל תַּחַת הַשָּׁמֶשׁ:

9:9 Enjoy life with a person you love all the fleeting days of the life that God has given you beneath the sun—all your fleeting days. That is what you get from life and from all your exertions beneath the sun.

While the text says, "Enjoy life with a *woman* you love," we have made it gender neutral because we believe that it reflects the sentiment of the verse. It should be noted that the first clause of this verse seems to contradict 7:26. Again, we are faced with a question as to what the writer or editor had in mind when including both verses. Was Kohelet repeating two competing truisms or proverbs? Did he change his mind, having written one observation in his youth and the second from the perspective of maturity? Perhaps this verse is the work of an editor who wanted to reshape what was previously included in the text. The *Targum* takes this verse literally, while Rashi considers it to be a metaphor for learning a trade. The *y'mei hevlecha*, "your fleeting days," reflect Kohelet and his melancholy, a stark reminder that life is short and essentially without meaning.

טוי כֹּל אֲשֶׁר תִּמְצָא יָדְךָ לַעֲשׂוֹת בְּכֹחֲךָ עֲשֵׂה כִּי אֵין מַעֲשֶׂה וְחֶשְׁבּוֹן
וְדַעַת וְחָכְמָה בִּשְׁאוֹל אֲשֶׁר אַתָּה הֹלֵךְ שָׁמָּה:

9:10 WHATEVER YOU CAN DO, DO IT WITH ALL YOUR MIGHT, BECAUSE IN *SH'OL*, WHERE YOU ARE GOING, THERE IS NEITHER ACTION, REASONING, KNOWLEDGE, NOR WISDOM.

Again, the same notion is repeated. Live life to the fullest. Make the most of it. Live it up while you live, since death is the end of everything. Such a thought, now emphasized over the course of several verses, seems to contravene traditional religious views. Kohelet does not even speak of immortality through children, as the reader would have expected in the context of the Bible. Hence, the *Targum* understands the verse to refer to the righteous who achieve their good works before they die so that they may receive their reward for them after death. Rashi, taking *cheshbon* as "accounting," tells the reader that the righteous need not be concerned about "accounting" in the world-to-come, but the wicked should be very concerned about it.

טויא שַׁבְתִּי וְרָאֹה תַחַת־הַשֶּׁמֶשׁ כִּי לֹא לַקַּלִּים הַמֵּרוֹץ וְלֹא לַגִּבּוֹרִים
הַמִּלְחָמָה וְגַם לֹא לַחֲכָמִים לֶחֶם וְגַם לֹא לַנְּבֹנִים עֹשֶׁר וְגַם לֹא
לַיֹּדְעִים חֵן כִּי־עֵת וָפֶגַע יִקְרֶה אֶת־כֻּלָּם:

9:11 AGAIN I SAW THAT BENEATH THE SUN THE RACE IS NOT WON BY THE SWIFT NOR THE BATTLE BY THE BRAVE, NOR IS BREAD GOTTEN BY THE WISE NOR WEALTH ACHIEVED BY THE INTELLIGENT NOR FAVOR ATTAINED BY THE LEARNED, BUT TIME AND CHANCE HAPPEN TO EVERYONE.

We follow Ibn Ezra in the translation of *kulam* as "everyone." The message here is simple: things just happen. It does not matter who you are or what you know. We may do our best, but we have no real control over the events in our lives. Kohelet seems to be saying that everything depends on luck. Do the most of what you can do, and do not think that the other person has more or that you could have won the race. If you were richer or stronger, or you could run faster, you would still not be better off, because it ultimately makes no difference. No matter how much another person accumulates, that person will still end up with nothing.

ט:יב כִּי גַּם לֹא־יֵדַע הָאָדָם אֶת־עִתּוֹ כַּדָּגִים שֶׁנֶּאֱחָזִים בִּמְצוֹדָה רָעָה וְכַצִּפֳּרִים הָאֲחֻזוֹת בַּפָּח כָּהֵם יוּקָשִׁים בְּנֵי הָאָדָם לְעֵת רָעָה כְּשֶׁתִּפּוֹל עֲלֵיהֶם פִּתְאֹם:

9:12 NO ONE KNOWS WHEN THAT TIME WILL COME. BUT LIKE FISH CAUGHT IN A DEADLY NET, OR LIKE BIRDS HELD FAST IN A SNARE, SO ARE HUMANS TRAPPED WHEN THAT FATAL MOMENT SUDDENLY DESCENDS UPON THEM.

"Time" is understood by the *Targum* as what is determined *b'mazaleihon*, "by their constellations." *Eit raah* is the time of death. Fish are caught in a net into which they unknowingly swim, and birds are trapped either by nets into which they can fly but from which they cannot escape or by enclosures into which they may fly but that fall and trap them. Kohelet uses such devices as similes of fate: however we go on the path of life, whether we watch where we go or not, when our time comes to die, we are powerless to resist its grasp.

ט:יג גַּם־זֹה רָאִיתִי חָכְמָה תַּחַת הַשָּׁמֶשׁ וּגְדוֹלָה הִיא אֵלָי:

9:13 ALSO THIS I NOTICED ABOUT WISDOM BENEATH THE SUN AND IT BOTHERED ME.

Kohelet notes what most of us have already observed in our own lives: wisdom, though it merits praise, often lacks it.

ט:יד עִיר קְטַנָּה וַאֲנָשִׁים בָּהּ מְעָט וּבָא־אֵלֶיהָ מֶלֶךְ גָּדוֹל וְסָבַב אֹתָהּ וּבָנָה עָלֶיהָ מְצוֹדִים גְּדֹלִים:

9:14 THERE WAS A SMALL CITY WITH FEW INHABITANTS, AND AGAINST IT CAME A GREAT SOVEREIGN. THE RULER SURROUNDED IT AND BUILT LARGE SIEGE MOUNDS AGAINST IT.

Ibn Ezra notes that earlier commentators, of whom Rashi was one, took the story of the "small city" as a parable. The "small city" represents the human body. The "few inhabitants" represent the bodily capacities serving the soul. The "sovereign" represents the evil inclination. The "poor but wise person" (in 9:15) represents the intellect. Following the *Targum,* Rashi holds that the "poor but wise person" is the good inclination. However, Ibn Ezra disagrees with this interpretation and thinks that the verse should be taken literally, reflecting a real event.

טו:טו וּמָצָא בָהּ אִישׁ מִסְכֵּן חָכָם וּמִלַּט־הוּא אֶת־הָעִיר בְּחָכְמָתוֹ וְאָדָם
לֹא זָכַר אֶת־הָאִישׁ הַמִּסְכֵּן הַהוּא:

9:15 In that city there happened to be a poor but wise person who, by his [or her] wisdom, might have saved the city. Alas, nobody mentioned that poor person.

This seems like a simple verse, but it is difficult to translate and interpret. There is a challenge with the connection between two words in this verse and the connection of this verse to the next one. The two words are *umilat* and *zachar*. If we take *umilat* as a past tense "and he saved, delivered" and we take *zachar* as "he remembered," we are then presented with the challenge of connecting the meaning of the two words as in the translation: "In that city there happened to be a poor but wise person who, by his wisdom, saved the city. Yet, no one remembered him." One has the sense that the unfortunate fate of the poor person would be better rendered by the present tense: "Yet no one remembers him." If this is the meaning of the verse, it is difficult to make a connection between 9:15 and 9:16, which says that the poor person's wisdom was not *used.* However, Ibn Ezra suggests a better translation of both words and makes a better connection to the next verse. On the basis of its use in Genesis 40:23, he translates *zachar* as "mention" and *umilat* as the *vav* consecutive "he will save, deliver." As may be seen above, our translation follows Ibn Ezra and makes a better connection with the next verse.

טו:טז וְאָמַרְתִּי אָנִי טוֹבָה חָכְמָה מִגְּבוּרָה וְחָכְמַת הַמִּסְכֵּן בְּזוּיָה וּדְבָרָיו
אֵינָם נִשְׁמָעִים:

9:16 Although I had said, "Wisdom is better than power," the poor person's wisdom was spurned and his [or her] words were not heard.

Here Kohelet contrasts a proverb with what really happens. Perhaps Kohelet's life experience changed his perspective from his younger days. Often it is not what you know, but whom you know. The poor person, because he was poor, could not get a hearing for plans that would have saved the city.

ט:יז דִּבְרֵי חֲכָמִים בְּנַחַת נִשְׁמָעִים מִזַּעֲקַת מוֹשֵׁל בַּכְּסִילִים:

9:17 THE WORDS OF THE WISE HEARD QUIETLY ARE BETTER
THAN THE RANTING OF A LEADER OF FOOLS.

Another apparently simple—but difficult—verse. The difficulty lies in the word
b'nachat, which could mean either "with quietness, quietly" or "with pleasure."
The *Targum* takes the first option for translation; Rashi takes the second. Interpreting
the words affects what is being contrasted. In other words, is it the sound made
or the persons making it? If we take the *Targum*'s view, then it is the quiet sound
of the words of "the wise" being contrasted with the *zaakat*, "shrieking, ranting," of
the "fools" and their leader. If we take Rashi's view, then it is the "wise" whose words
are accepted with pleasure as against whatever is said by the "fools." For the *Targum*,
God is the one listening to the words of the wise in prayer. For Rashi, it is the people
of Israel who still hearken to the words of Moses. It may be a coincidence or a matter
of style, but Kohelet used the last word of the previous verse, *nishmaim* (to be heard),
in this verse, as if the use of the word above reminded him to use it here.

ט:יח טוֹבָה חָכְמָה מִכְּלֵי קְרָב וְחוֹטֶא אֶחָד יְאַבֵּד טוֹבָה הַרְבֵּה:

9:18 WISDOM IS BETTER THAN WEAPONS, BUT ONE SINNER
CAN DESTROY MUCH GOOD.

Either we are dealing with two separate proverbs, here joined accidentally, or *choteh*
(sinner) does not mean what it usually does but rather "one who makes a mistake"
or "mistake." Unless we assume that many of the verses in this text are random
jottings made by Kohelet during his lifetime, such a conclusion is required, since the
notions of "wisdom" and "sinner" seem to occupy different worlds. Unmoved by
issues of consistency, the *Targum* and Rashi take *choteh* to mean "sinner." Ibn Ezra
relates the word to the "ruler of fools" in the previous verse.

Hezekiah

King Hezekiah reigned as king of Judah from 727 to 698 B.C.E. He was described in
the Bible as a righteous king who instituted religious reform that included the
eradication of idolatry, the cleansing of the Temple, and the restoration of the Temple
cult. These actions were influenced by the prophet Isaiah. For the sake of political
independence, he rebelled against the king of Assyria, Sennacherib, who laid siege to
Jerusalem as a result. In order to prepare the city for an assault, he built a (still extant)
tunnel from the Gihon spring to bring water into the city. While the city was spared
because of a plague that affected the Assyrian army, Sennacherib nevertheless exacted a
large tribute from Hezekiah for the revolt.

White Garments

While white garments may be a sign of wealth (since laborers would be unable to wear white), they also have religious significance. In particular, the *kittel* (Yiddish for "gown") is seen at weddings or a Passover meal, generally among Orthodox or traditional Jews. This full-length, large white outer garment is also what the individual is dressed in for burial. Its most common use is among men who wear it to the synagogue on Rosh HaShanah and Yom Kippur. In some synagogues, the *kittel* has been replaced by a white clergy robe that resembles a judge's robe. White symbolizes purity and, with purity, the repentance of past sins. In some communities, the *kittel* is also worn on the eighth day of Sukkot (when the traditional prayer for rain is recited) and on the first day of Passover (when the prayer for dew is recited). And in most synagogues, the garments that adorn the Torah, the ark covering, and the reading table are changed to white during the High Holy Days to represent a rebirth and a cleanliness from the stain of sin.

Vav *Consecutive*

This is a grammatical form that is a hallmark of biblical Hebrew. When the *vav* (the conjunction "and") is added to a verb, it changes a future tense to past tense. While there may have been some early distinction between a *vav* consecutive and a *vav* conversive, the terms are generally used interchangeably.

GLEANINGS

The Growth of Wisdom

Perhaps by framing Sarah's age at the time of her death . . . the Torah text is suggesting that Sarah's wisdom grew from year to year. This growth in wisdom resulted from what she gained in life experience in each succeeding year. Sarah then applied that learning to the year that followed, producing an accumulated effect after such a long life. Thus, unlike others who might have reached the same age simply through the amassing of years, Sarah gained the wisdom which our tradition seems to unconditionally ascribe to older people, a posture that post-modern western culture generally seems to eschew.

For young, middle-aged, or old, there is a powerful lesson here for us to learn. Sarah provides us with a wonderful model of how one navigates her way through the challenges of life and learns to grow beyond them. She exemplifies what I have observed in many people as they age. It seems that people don't change as they get older—unless they get on the path of *teshuva*. (Commentators like the Sefat Emet suggest that Sarah's growth in wisdom was indeed a result of her constant practice of *teshuva*.) Instead, older people are the same as younger people, *only more so*. The characteristics that we exhibit intensify with each passing year—so we have to make sure that we are who we will always want to be.

Kerry M. Olitzky, "Chaye Sarah" (Electronic Beit Midrash, Wexner Heritage Foundation, November 1999)

The Satisfaction of Work

In freely admitting that you work not necessarily because you *want* to but because you *have* to, you have one of two choices.

You can slough off and try to "just get by," doing as little as possible in order to get your paycheck.

Or you can give yourself the opportunity to derive great *personal* meaning and fulfillment from your work.

For you can work not for "outside" recognition, not for "outside" approval, but for "inner" satisfaction, for "inner" reward.

You can have the satisfaction of knowing that you do the very, very best job you can do. You can have the integrity and the joy of knowing that you give 100 percent of your energy, your capability, your dedication, to your work.

If you mop floors, you can have the cleanest floors. If you design rocket boosters, you can have the most meticulous drawings. If you stock shelves, you can have the straightest displays. If you attach car doors on an assembly line, you can align the doors perfectly. If you manage multi-million-dollar stock portfolios, you can buy and sell with total integrity. If you clean houses, you can have the neatest houses on the block.

If you are part of a work team, you can contribute your very best work, for you know that a team is only as strong as its weakest member. The orchestra produces magnificent sound only when every instrument is played precisely by every musician. The chorus produces beautiful music only when every singer hits each note in perfect harmony. Your team, your unit, your division, can produce and succeed only when you give your best skills and your strongest commitment.

Everything depends on you being sure that you are doing your best.

For when you bring to your work your best effort, you can derive the most satisfaction.

Wayne Dosick, *The Business Bible: Ten Commandments for Creating an Ethical Workplace* (New York: William Morrow and Company, 1993), 158–59

My Father's Death

My father died a good death. He said good-bye to the people he loved and made his wishes known. His end was peaceful and dignified. Yet, even though I knew it was coming, the shock of his death was staggering. The world that I had known was gone and I would never be the same. A friend who lives above the San Andreas Fault in Los Angeles described the feeling as "a private earthquake."

During the days and weeks following my father's death, I explored the quiet devastation left by his loss. I assumed a new role and became a mourner. As lonely as I was without my dad, I was not alone. My family and my community comforted me, and I felt myself traveling down a path made smooth by centuries of Jewish mourners. . . .

My father's death taught me the meaning of the word "blessing." His memory is a palpable blessing in my life, a reminder to stay in touch with beauty, to be kind, to laugh.

His death also taught me new lessons about the blessings of Jewish ritual and community. The structure of Jewish tradition (sitting *shiva*, setting the first month apart, attending services to say Kaddish, counting myself among the mourners) guided me though dark days. I explored new depths of connection to the synagogue where I had been a member for eighteen years. The outpouring of support and affection from members of Congregation Beth El of the Sudbury River Valley was due not simply to the presence of compassionate individuals in the congregation; the communal response to my loss was rooted in the ancient, holy requirement—the *mitzvah*—that Jews comfort the bereaved.

Anita Diamant, *Saying Kaddish: How to Comfort the Dying, Bury the Dead, and Mourn as a Jew*
(New York: Schocken Books, 1998), xv, xvii

CHAPTER TEN

י:א זְבוּבֵי מָוֶת יַבְאִישׁ יַבִּיעַ שֶׁמֶן רוֹקֵחַ יָקָר מֵחָכְמָה מִכָּבוֹד סִכְלוּת
מְעָט:

10:1 AS DEAD FLIES PUTRIFY A PERFUMER'S OIL, SO A LITTLE
FOLLY OUTWEIGHS MUCH WISDOM.

A rotten apple spoils the bunch. The English word "putrify" renders two Hebrew
words *yavish* (makes stink) and *yabia* (makes bubble up). Just as it takes only a few
dead flies to destroy perfume, so it takes just a little folly to destroy the work of
wisdom. The *Targum* takes the verse as a parable describing the work of the evil
inclination. It seems that this verse and the others that follow in this chapter are a
collection of somewhat random proverbs and sayings that do not have much
connection of one to another.

י:ב לֵב חָכָם לִימִינוֹ וְלֵב כְּסִיל לִשְׂמֹאלוֹ:

10:2 A WISE PERSON'S MIND IS ONE'S FORTUNE. A FOOL'S
MIND IS ONE'S MISFORTUNE.

The literal meanings of the words *limino* (to his right hand) and *lismolo* (to his left
hand) are translated as "one's fortune" and "one's misfortune," because in many
places those who are right-handed are considered to be more fortunate than those
who are left-handed. Note, for example, the naming of Benjamin (Genesis 35:18),
in which the name Ben-oni, "Son of My Suffering," is changed to "Son of the Right
Hand," and the Latin word *sinistra* (left hand), which underlies the word "sinister."
The *Targum* explains that the wise person seeks to acquire Torah learning that
was given *b'yad y'mina dAdonai* (by the right hand of Adonai), while the fool
seeks merely possessions of silver and gold. Rashi also takes the right hand as
indicative of the proper path one should follow and the left hand as that which
leads away from the proper path. Ibn Ezra informs his readers that *lev* (literally,
"heart"), which we have translated as "mind," cannot mean "heart," because the
heart is in the middle of the body. Rather, the term refers to *haseichel* (the mind).
"Right" and "left" are metaphors. As the right hand has more strength and more
agility than the left hand for those who are right-handed, so the mind of the wise
is more acute than the mind of the fool. Ibn Ezra tells us that such metaphorical
use is found among many people.

י:ג וְגַם־בַּדֶּרֶךְ כשהסכל כְּשֶׁסָּכָל הֹלֵךְ לִבּוֹ חָסֵר וְאָמַר לַכֹּל סָכָל הוּא:

10:3 EVEN WHEN A FOOL TRAVELS, THE MIND IS NOT THERE
[WITH HIM], AND SO HE ANNOUNCES TO EVERYBODY
THAT HE IS A FOOL.

Folly is linked not to a place but to a person. Ibn Ezra notes that in everything
that fools do, they manifest their lack of intellect and lack of knowledge. Even
"on the road," a fool is a fool.

י:ד אִם־רוּחַ הַמּוֹשֵׁל תַּעֲלֶה עָלֶיךָ מְקוֹמְךָ אַל־תַּנַּח כִּי מַרְפֵּא יַנִּיחַ
חֲטָאִים גְּדוֹלִים:

10:4 IF THE RULER SHOULD RAGE AGAINST YOU, DON'T
ABANDON YOUR POSITION. CALM MAY ASSUAGE GREAT
FAULTS.

Another seemingly simple but difficult verse. *Marpei* in the last clause poses the initial
problem. If it is derived from *rapei* [r-p-(alef)], then the word means "healing." It may
have a second meaning of "remedy" according to Koehler and Baumgartner (p. 637).
If it is derived from *rafeh* [r-f-(hei)], then the word means "calm" or "gentleness."
Chataim is the other troublesome word in the last clause. It can mean either a "sin"
against God or an "offense, fault" against humans. *Tanach* in the second clause and
yaniach in the last clause come from the same root *nuach* (to rest) and have related
meanings in the *hifil* verb form. In the first case, it means "to let go of, to abandon,"
and in the second case, it means to "undo offenses" (according to Koehler and
Baumgartner, p. 680). We have taken *marpei* to mean "calm," *tanach* to mean
"abandon," and *yaniach* to mean "undo offenses, assuage." The relation of the last
clause to the first suggests that this verse is like the advice given in the Book of
Proverbs (e.g., 23:1; 25:5–8; 29:26): how to succeed in government. The *Targum*
takes *marpei* as "healing" and *chataim* as "sins." It understands "the ruler" as the
evil inclination, which wishes to remove the individual from one's proper place.
There is hope for such an individual because the words of Torah can heal the many
sins that the evil inclination incited.

י:ה יֵשׁ רָעָה רָאִיתִי תַּחַת הַשָּׁמֶשׁ כִּשְׁגָגָה שֶׁיֹּצָא מִלִּפְנֵי הַשַּׁלִּיט:

10:5 THERE IS SOMETHING WRONG THAT I HAVE SEEN
BENEATH THE SUN, WHICH IS LIKE A BLUNDER COMING
FROM SOMEONE IN CHARGE.

Kohelet makes the point that those who rule are expected to—and should know—
what they are doing. Just as we expect professionals, of whatever kind, to know
their professions, we expect our rulers to be competent. An incompetent ruler,

like an ignorant scholar, should be an oxymoron. Yet, as the next verse indicates, such contradictions exist.

נִתַּן הַסֶּכֶל בַּמְּרוֹמִים רַבִּים וַעֲשִׁירִים בַּשֵּׁפֶל יֵשֵׁבוּ: י:ו

10:6 FOLLY IS SET IN THE HIGHEST HEIGHTS, WHILE THE RICH DWELL AT THE LOWEST LEVEL.

In the natural order of things, one would expect folly to be set on low and wisdom to be set on high. Wealth, one would expect, would find its own level. Here Kohelet complains that the reality of the world confounds both sense and cynicism: folly wins and wealth does not. One cannot even depend on the wrong things happening.

רָאִיתִי עֲבָדִים עַל־סוּסִים וְשָׂרִים הֹלְכִים כַּעֲבָדִים עַל־הָאָרֶץ: י:ז

10:7 I HAVE SEEN SLAVES RIDING ON HORSES AND PRINCES WALKING ON THE GROUND LIKE SLAVES.

Kohelet's complaint about the inversion of social expectations suggests his position in society. Had he been one of the ''slaves,'' he probably would not have complained. Both the *Targum* and Rashi understand the verse as Solomon's anticipatory comment on the Chaldean invasion described in Isaiah 23.

חֹפֵר גּוּמָץ בּוֹ יִפּוֹל וּפֹרֵץ גָּדֵר יִשְּׁכֶנּוּ נָחָשׁ: י:ח

10:8 THE ONE WHO DIGS A PIT MAY FALL INTO IT. THE ONE WHO BREAKS DOWN A FENCE MAY BE BITTEN BY A SNAKE.

Kohelet seems to be quoting a proverb that deals with what is called ''the law of unintended consequences.'' The verse suggests that any change may be bad, perhaps even worse than the present situation is. Such a conservative view reflects satisfaction with the status quo. Generally, it is the ''haves'' who are satisfied with what is; it is the ''have nots'' who are dissatisfied.

מַסִּיעַ אֲבָנִים יֵעָצֵב בָּהֶם בּוֹקֵעַ עֵצִים יִסָּכֶן בָּם: י:ט

10:9 ONE WHO QUARRIES ROCKS MAY BE HURT BY THEM. ONE WHO SPLITS WOOD MAY BE ENDANGERED.

The aspects of building, as described by Kohelet, suggest a different nuance to the notion presented by the preceding verse. Even when one consciously does something positive, it may have a negative result. We follow Rashi in translating *masia* as ''quarries'' and Ibn Ezra in translating *yisachen* as ''may be endangered.''

יׄי אִם־קֵהָה הַבַּרְזֶל וְהוּא לֹא־פָנִים קִלְקַל וַחֲיָלִים יְגַבֵּר וְיִתְרוֹן הַכְשֵׁיר חָכְמָה:

10:10 IF THE AXE HEAD IS DULL AND ITS EDGE HAS NOT BEEN SHARPENED, THEN YOU MUST EXERT YOURSELF ALL THE MORE. HENCE, WISDOM TAKES ADVANTAGE OF PREPARATION.

The simple message: sharpen your tools so that you do not have to work as hard. But the precise translation of the verse is not so simple. On the basis of the possible usage of *panim* in Ezekiel 21:21, the word is interpreted to mean "the sharp edge of a sword" by Koehler and Baumgartner (p. 940); hence, we have translated it as "edge." However, the Kittel Bible, a scholarly critical edition of the Hebrew text that compares various manuscript versions, proposes an emendation to *lo l'fanim,* which would change the meaning to "not beforehand." Even so, the sense of the first clause so far would remain the same, since "and its edge has not been sharpened" assumes "beforehand," that is, before the using of the axe head. *Vachayalim y'gabeir,* the last two words of the first clause, are taken by the *Targum* and Rashi to mean "God will confer victory to [God's] soldiers," that is, in spite of deficient virtue (the *Targum*) or deficient weaponry (Rashi). They are taken by Ibn Ezra and by Koehler and Baumgartner (p. 311) as "to exert strength." Even more problematic are the three words of the last clause, *v'yitron hachsheir chochmah.* Each of these three words make sense alone: *v'yitron* (and the benefit), *hachsheir* (preparation), and *chochmah* (wisdom, skill). It is the joining of the three that is challenging. Perhaps what is suggested is that the mark of a professional, one who has the "skill," is that that person prepares in advance, while the non-professional does not do so. Such a suggested meaning would be better were the word order *v'yitron chochmah hachsheir.*

יׄיא אִם־יִשֹּׁךְ הַנָּחָשׁ בְּלוֹא־לָחַשׁ וְאֵין יִתְרוֹן לְבַעַל הַלָּשׁוֹן:

10:11 IF A SNAKE WILL BITE WITHOUT BEING CHARMED, THERE IS NO ADVANTAGE IN BEING A SNAKE CHARMER.

In this verse, Kohelet uses the same word (*yitron,* "advantage") that he did in the previous verse. Such repetition may have been a method for preserving texts by memory. It is not clear by the verse for what purpose the "snake" was "being charmed." Ibn Ezra thinks that the snake was being charmed *to* bite. Rashi thinks that it was being charmed *not* to bite. In either case, the snake charmer lost out, because the snake struck before the services of the snake charmer were required. In this verse Kohelet offers another example in which knowledge is *not* power.

י:יב דִּבְרֵי פִי־חָכָם חֵן וְשִׂפְתוֹת כְּסִיל תְּבַלְּעֶנּוּ:

10:12 THE WORDS OF THE WISE FIND GRACE, BUT THE LIPS
OF THE FOOL WILL ENGULF HIM [OR HER].

The *Targum* takes the verse literally, that is, when deserved destruction comes upon a wicked generation, a wise person can pray, asking for divine mercy, and thus save that generation. Fools, on the other hand, can bring destruction on themselves and the entire generation just by saying the wrong things.

י:יג תְּחִלַּת דִּבְרֵי־פִיהוּ סִכְלוּת וְאַחֲרִית פִּיהוּ הוֹלֵלוּת רָעָה:

10:13 THE FOOL'S SPEECH AT THE BEGINNING IS
FOOLISHNESS AND AT THE END IS TOTAL MADNESS.

Ibn Ezra comments that a fool's speech makes no sense from beginning to end. Even so, the lack of sense does not stop the fool.

י:יד וְהַסָּכָל יַרְבֶּה דְבָרִים לֹא־יֵדַע הָאָדָם מַה־שֶׁיִּהְיֶה וַאֲשֶׁר יִהְיֶה
מֵאַחֲרָיו מִי יַגִּיד לוֹ:

10:14 YET THE FOOL KEEPS TALKING. NO ONE KNOWS
WHAT WILL BE. WHO CAN TELL ANYONE WHAT THE
FUTURE HOLDS?

Although the *Targum*, Rashi, and Ibn Ezra take the entire verse as one unit, Gordis (*Wisdom of Ecclesiastes*, p. 314) has taken the last clause as a separate notion. Humans cannot know what will happen. Who will tell people what happened before, since most people who lived previously have died and most people will not listen to those who are still alive? Rashi takes this verse to refer to Balaam, hired to curse the people of Israel and so destroy them, but who was himself destroyed in the end.

י:טו עֲמַל הַכְּסִילִים תְּיַגְּעֶנּוּ אֲשֶׁר לֹא־יָדַע לָלֶכֶת אֶל־עִיר:

10:15 A FOOL'S EFFORTS ARE TIRING, FOR THE FOOL DOES
NOT EVEN KNOW HOW TO GET TO THE CITY.

The individual does not know in which direction to go. The last part of this verse may be a proverb, or both verses may be proverbs quoted by Kohelet. Perhaps these are simple notebook jottings of Kohelet as the old professor that we have seen throughout this book. The *Targum* adds that in the city dwell the wise, who might have been able to provide the fool with instruction. Rashi adds that not knowing the proper entrances to the city, the fool sinks into mire.

י:טז אִי־לָךְ אֶרֶץ שֶׁמַּלְכֵּךְ נָעַר וְשָׂרַיִךְ בַּבֹּקֶר יֹאכֵלוּ:

10:16 WOE TO YOU, O LAND, WHOSE RULER IS BUT A CHILD
AND WHOSE PRINCES EAT WHILE IT IS YET MORNING.

This is a difficult verse, particularly when coupled with the verse that follows. Although the first clause seems simple, the understanding of the word *naar* is problematic. It can mean either "lad" or "servant." If it means lad or child, the complaint is that the ruler is immature—in terms of either age or behavior. If *naar* means servant, the verse makes a better contrast with the one that follows. There the ruler is described as being *ben chorin* (child of nobles, nobly born). Thus, the ruler is a member of the elite. It is not clear what may be the error of the princes. It is that they should be working—and not eating—in the morning. Perhaps they are like contemporary adolescents: getting up late and just eating breakfast when half the workday is already done. The verse that follows tells us that the princes of the "happy" land "eat at a proper time." Apparently, such a time is not in the morning. The *Targum* applies this verse to the reign of Jeroboam ben Navat. He was the king, whether immature or ill-born is not made clear, whose ministers ate breakfast before offering the *tamid* sacrifice. Rashi understands the verse more generally: "woe to the land" whose rulers and judges act childishly. Ibn Ezra understands the "child" to refer to the ruler who is a fool; whether folly is a function of age or social standing is not made clear.

י:יז אַשְׁרֵיךְ אֶרֶץ שֶׁמַּלְכֵּךְ בֶּן־חוֹרִים וְשָׂרַיִךְ בָּעֵת יֹאכֵלוּ בִּגְבוּרָה
וְלֹא בַשְּׁתִי:

10:17 HAPPY ARE YOU, O LAND, WHOSE RULER IS NOBLY
BORN AND WHOSE PRINCES EAT AT A PROPER TIME AND
DO SO WITH SELF-CONTROL AND NOT WHILE DRUNK.

G'vurah, which usually means "power" or "strength," here presents a problem: with which kind of power or strength do these princes eat? According to the *Targum*, it is *bigvurat oraita* (with the power of Torah). According to Rashi, it is with the power of wisdom. But for Koehler and Baumgartner (p. 172), it is with self-control.

י:יח בַּעֲצַלְתַּיִם יִמַּךְ הַמְּקָרֶה וּבְשִׁפְלוּת יָדַיִם יִדְלֹף הַבָּיִת:

10:18 BECAUSE OF LAZINESS, THE CEILING FALLS IN. IDLE
HANDS MAKE THE HOUSE LEAK.

The simple message of the verse: take precautions. As any homeowner knows, if you don't repair the roof when you should, you will pay for it later. This is also true if you don't repair the walls. This verse seems to be another proverb quoted by Kohelet or an observation he has made during his lifetime. The reader will remember that Kohelet questioned the efficacy of any endeavor in previous verses (9:11; 10:8–11).

י:יט לִשְׂחוֹק עֹשִׂים לֶחֶם וְיַיִן יְשַׂמַּח חַיִּים וְהַכֶּסֶף יַעֲנֶה אֶת־הַכֹּל:

10:19 THEY MAKE BANQUETS FOR PLEASURE, AND WINE MAKES PEOPLE HAPPY, BUT MONEY MAKES IT ALL POSSIBLE.

Based on the usage of *lechem* (literally, "bread") in Daniel 5:1, Rashi understands it to mean bread as "banquet." The *Targum* reads the verse as a reference to the righteous providing for the poor. Ibn Ezra understands *yaaneh* (literally, "will answer") as *yamtzi* (brings into being).

י:כ גַּם בְּמַדָּעֲךָ מֶלֶךְ אַל־תְּקַלֵּל וּבְחַדְרֵי מִשְׁכָּבְךָ אַל־תְּקַלֵּל עָשִׁיר כִּי עוֹף הַשָּׁמַיִם יוֹלִיךְ אֶת־הַקּוֹל וּבַעַל הכנפים כְּנָפַיִם יַגֵּיד דָּבָר:

10:20 EVEN IN YOUR MIND, DON'T CURSE A RULER. EVEN IN YOUR BOREDOM, DON'T CURSE A RICH PERSON. FOR A HEAVENLY BIRD WILL BRING A REPORT AND ONE WITH WINGS TO TELL THE STORY.

The simple message of the verse: be prudent. This appears to be another of Kohelet's sayings. The *Targum*, Rashi, and Ibn Ezra agree that the meaning of the unfamiliar word *b'madaacha* is "in your mind, in your thoughts." To explain what "ruler" could know what is in a person's mind, Rashi understands the ruler to be "the Ruler of rulers" and the "heavenly bird" to be the human soul, which ultimately will fly up to heaven, and the "one with wings" to be the angel that will accompany the individual on the flight to heaven. Ibn Ezra takes the verse more literally. He suggests that if you curse either "a ruler" or "a rich person," word will get out and rulers can harm you by sovereign power or, in the case of the rich person, can harm you with their wealth.

Balaam

According to the Torah (Numbers 22–24), Balak, the king of Moab, asked Balaam (in Hebrew, *Bil'am*), a pagan seer, to curse the Israelites as they made their way to Canaan through the desert. Under divine inspiration, he was able to utter only words of praise. Some of his words, which include the familiar "How goodly are your tents O Jacob, your dwelling places O Israel" (Num. 24:5) have made their way into the daily service and are traditionally said upon entering the synagogue each morning for prayer. One of Balaam's statements, "A star shall come forth from Jacob, and a scepter shall rise out of Israel" (Num. 24:17), was taken as a messianic prediction and applied to Shimon bar Kochba, leader of the second revolt against Rome (132–135 C.E.).

The Tamid *Sacrifice*

The daily burnt offering in the ancient Temple in Jerusalem, whose laws are described in Numbers 28:1–6, is called the *olah tamid,* or "perpetual sacrifice." There we are told that the sacrifice consists of "two first-year lambs without blemish, day by day, for a continual burnt offering. One lamb you shall offer in the morning, and the other lamb you shall offer in the evening..." (Numbers 28:3–4).

GLEANINGS

Slavery Is Bad

There is a message in the Passover story that any cultural group could well afford to comprehend. It's simple: Slavery is bad; freedom is good. These two opposite conditions are contemplated by the Passover story in every dimension—physical as well as spiritual. An old Hasidic proverb reminds us that "the real slavery in Egypt was that they had leaned to endure it." A poem from England intuitively tells us: "My very chains and I grew friends / So much a long communion tends / To make us what we are." ...

When Moses went into Pharaoh's court and demanded freedom for the slaves, he was speaking for every nation and for every epoch. This was the first time, in the recorded history of humankind, that any cultural group had demanded and eventually got a deliverance from the confines of another cultural group. This is also the first recorded religious tradition alleging that even the heavens intervened in the matter of slavery versus freedom. Over and over again the Bible tells us that God "heard the cries of the Hebrews." Whether or not you interpret the scriptural assertion literally, the fact remains that this is the original saga linking the intention of heaven with the direction of earth. And, indeed, Moses was the world's first civil rights leader, and the Hebrew exodus from Egypt was the world's first national liberation movement. No wonder that many American Jews, among other good and courageous people, identified with Dr. Martin Luther King's social revolution of a generation ago.

Ben Kamin, *Thinking Passover: A Rabbi's Book of Holiday Values* (New York: Dutton, 1997), 59–60

Making Room for God in Your Success

In Deuteronomy 8, Moses told the Israelites that after their forty-year trek through the wilderness they were about to enter "a land where you may eat food without stint, where you will lack nothing."

"When you have eaten your fill," he said, "and have built fine houses to live in, and your herds and flocks have multiplied, and your silver and gold have increased, and everything you own has prospered, beware lest your heart grow haughty and you forget the Eternal your God...and you say to yourselves, 'My own power and the might of my hand have won this wealth for me.' Remember that it is the Eternal your God who gives you the power to get wealth, in fulfillment of the covenant that He made on oath with your fathers, as is still the case.''

Even thousands of years ago, Moses knew that each of us is tempted by arrogance and selfishness, by vain assumptions that we are the sole progenitors of all that we do. The wisdom he spoke of on the eve of his people's entry into Israel still rings true. Its credence and force have a place in every shop and office and boardroom in late-20th-century America, in every business deal and artistic endeavor, in every ride we take in the elevator that carries us to yet another work day or every time we sit down in the pickup truck in which we ride on our appointed rounds.

Like the people of ancient Israel, we have built fine houses and our silver and gold have multiplied. Undeniably, we have prospered in many ways. But the price of that prosperity is a poverty of the soul. It is time to be as rich internally as we are externally; to be as rooted in the divine as we are in the material; to know that, as Moses said, it is God who gives us the power to acquire wealth, and that it is God who also gives us sustenance, to Whom we owe obeisance and thanks—and Who we should remember gave us not just this day and its accomplishments, but all of them.

Jeffrey K. Salkin, *Being God's Partner: How to Find the Hidden Link Between Spirituality and Your Work* (Woodstock, Vt.: Jewish Lights Publishing, 1994), 175–76

Holy Time, Holy Space

An eternity glows within our mundane selves. Instinctively we sense that we are holy beings: *Ela'in Kadishin*. We are manufactured of sacred material. We are *b'tzelem elohim*—not gods, but God's image. Just as a photograph of a mountain is not the mountain itself but an image deposited by light in the presence of the actual mountain, so we suspect ourselves to be a finite image, *tzilum*, a snapshot, left by God's being in the presence of some infinite light. We are what is left after the infinite one has passed by here—a fossil in the cleft of the rock—and though we are frail and mortal, our imagination soars because we feel our ancient and eternal connection to that infinity that put us here.

These lofty thoughts envelop us at great sacred moments like *Kol Nidrey* or our wedding or our granddaughter's *bat mitzvah*. At these times the rituals ring true. The words celebrate the wonderfully obvious.

But on a random Wednesday in January it is harder for us to see ourselves as beings of divine light. Sometimes we would rather die than emerge from bed. We are so burdened with regrets, responsibilities, and, perhaps, physical maladies, that we cannot imagine facing another day of gloom.

Here the Jewish tradition tries to help:

It offers the prayer "You revive the dead with great mercy" to remind us that every day that we *choose* to go on living is a moment of encounter with the driving force of life itself. It is not the dead who are revived, but we the living who *feel* as if we are barely able to go on trying.

It enjoins us to utter words of recognition each time we pop something into our mouths. Simply by saying "Blessed are You who created this, Blessed are You who created that" we invite ourselves to link the mundane act of eating with the eternal source of nourishment.

It instructs us to leave the bathroom with the words "You created us wisely, with openings and closing without which we could not stand before you for a moment." Thus it reminds us to view any aspect of our bodies that functions properly as a cause for thanksgiving, as a moment of surprise akin to Jacob's discovery of a heavenly ladder in the midst of a desert.

But even these moments of blessing are somewhat "official" by virtue of the prescribed words we associate with them. We should also carry over our sense of the sacred to the mundane words and deeds of our workday and private lives. We can consider every interaction with associates, friends, or loved ones to be a playing out of the free will and trust that God gave us. We can examine the words that emerge from our mouths to determine whether or not a listener would perceive the image of God in us. We can look at the things we sell, the clients we represent, the assignments we accept, the ideas we proffer, to determine whether or not we are diminishing the world's sacredness or adding to it.

Lester Bronstein, "Holy Time, Holy Space," *Bulletin* (Bet Am Shalom Synagogue, White Plains, N.Y.), January 1993, 1

CHAPTER ELEVEN

יא:א שַׁלַּח לַחְמְךָ עַל־פְּנֵי הַמָּיִם כִּי־בְרֹב הַיָּמִים תִּמְצָאֶנּוּ:

11:1 SEND OUT YOUR BREAD ON THE WATERS, FOR AFTER
MANY DAYS YOU WILL FIND IT.

There seems to be no divine retribution. If you spread your bounty, you will be
rewarded. The *Targum* explains to whom "bread on the waters" is sent: *laaniyei
d'azlin bisfinan,* "to the poor who go on ships." What the benefactor will find is *agreih
l'alma d'atei,* "his reward in the world-to-come."

יא:ב תֶּן־חֵלֶק לְשִׁבְעָה וְגַם לִשְׁמוֹנָה כִּי לֹא תֵדַע מַה־יִּהְיֶה רָעָה
עַל־הָאָרֶץ:

11:2 GIVE A PORTION TO SEVEN OR EIGHT, BECAUSE YOU
CANNOT TELL WHAT EVIL WILL COME UPON THE
EARTH.

You never know when you will be in want. To be forewarned is to be forearmed.
The *Targum,* Rashi, and Ibn Ezra differ as to the meaning of "seven or eight." For
the *Targum,* they refer to the months of the year, starting with Nisan. The message is
for readers to sow in the month of Tishrei and even in the month of Kislev.
(Apparently, the month of Cheshvan was somehow omitted or did not exist in the
mind of the author of the *Targum.*) For Rashi, "seven or eight" refers to providing
for different needy persons or, quoting the Rabbis (Babylonian Talmud, *Eiruvin* 40b),
to the mitzvot of the Sabbath, ritual circumcision, or the paschal offering. For Ibn Ezra,
"seven or eight" is an idiom meaning "continually, without a break." Just as the
commentators differ in their explanation of the first clause of this verse, they differ
with regard to the second clause as well. The *Targum* explains "what evil will come
upon the earth" as *i charfei nitzhan,* "whether the blooms have early or late seeds."
Rashi explains the "evil" as the destruction of the Temple and the cessation of
the related sacrifices that bring rain, while Ibn Ezra explains that the phrase simply
means "poverty."

יא:ג אִם־יִמָּלְאוּ הֶעָבִים גֶּשֶׁם עַל־הָאָרֶץ יָרִיקוּ וְאִם־יִפּוֹל עֵץ בַּדָּרוֹם
וְאִם בַּצָּפוֹן מְקוֹם שֶׁיִּפּוֹל הָעֵץ שָׁם יְהוּא:

11:3 IF THE CLOUDS ARE FILLED WITH RAIN, THEY EMPTY IT
UPON THE EARTH. IF A TREE FALLS IN THE SOUTH OR
IN THE NORTH, WHERE IT FALLS, THERE IT REMAINS.

Kohelet suggests that there is cause and effect in this world. Certain things are inevitable, and you can see the signs. The *Targum* does not accept the possibility that this verse might suggest that natural events are beyond human control. Hence, the "clouds filled with rain" were due to *z'chuta d'tzadikaya*, "the merit of the righteous." Likewise, the "tree" that falls is a metaphor for a king being deposed. Such an event does not just happen; it is *itg'zar min sh'maya*, "divinely decreed." Rashi takes the first part of the verse as an indication of a logical process and the fallen tree in the second part of the verse as a metaphor for the lasting impact that a scholar can have on a community. Ibn Ezra, however, takes the first part of the verse as a metaphor for wealth and the second part as a metaphor for the results of wealth.

יא:ד שֹׁמֵר רוּחַ לֹא יִזְרָע וְרֹאֶה בֶעָבִים לֹא יִקְצוֹר:

11:4 THE ONE WHO WATCHES THE WIND WILL NEVER SOW,
AND THE ONE WHO GAZES AT THE CLOUDS WILL
NEVER REAP.

This is not a message to "stop and smell the roses." Rather, Kohelet wants his readers to know that there are times you have to act without thinking the action through to its logical conclusion. This too may be a proverb that Kohelet quotes to suggest that although nature may not be under human control, you must do what you can. Both the *Targum* and Ibn Ezra take this verse as a metaphor. The *Targum* maintains that it refers to one who depends on magic or upon the actions of constellations to guide one's actions. Ibn Ezra teaches that the verse refers to a benefactor who, in supporting a lazy person, causes a miser to view such an act of generosity as useless.

יא:ה כַּאֲשֶׁר אֵינְךָ יוֹדֵעַ מַה־דֶּרֶךְ הָרוּחַ כַּעֲצָמִים בְּבֶטֶן הַמְּלֵאָה כָּכָה
לֹא תֵדַע אֶת־מַעֲשֵׂה הָאֱלֹהִים אֲשֶׁר יַעֲשֶׂה אֶת־הַכֹּל:

11:5 JUST AS YOU DON'T KNOW THE WAY THAT BREATH
ENTERS BONES IN A PREGNANT WOMAN'S WOMB, SO
YOU DON'T KNOW WHAT GOD DOES, WHO DOES
EVERYTHING.

You really cannot be sure what God/chance/providence is going to provide. The power of this verse, and its import, are dependent on the meanings of the word *ruach* as "wind," "breath," or "life." The same meanings and the same connection of *ruach* to bones are found in Ezekiel 37:5 in the Dry Bones vision. In Ezekiel, *ruach* promises the revival of the dead. Here in Kohelet, *ruach* presents the embryonic origins of life.

יא:ו בַּבֹּקֶר זְרַע אֶת־זַרְעֶךָ וְלָעֶרֶב אַל־תַּנַּח יָדֶךָ כִּי אֵינְךָ יוֹדֵעַ אֵי זֶה
יִכְשָׁר הֲזֶה אוֹ־זֶה וְאִם־שְׁנֵיהֶם כְּאֶחָד טוֹבִים:

11:6 In the morning, sow your seed, but don't stop when it is evening, for you don't know which will turn out, this one or that one, or whether both will be good.

All you can do is to do your best in whatever you do. This statement is a rejection of passivity. Both the *Targum* and Rashi take the verse to be a metaphor about marriage. While certainly male-centered, they suggest that the reader marry a woman who can have children when he is young. If he is older, he should still marry a woman who can have children. Rashi also takes the verse to be a metaphor about the study of Torah. If you have studied Torah when you were young, continue to do so when you become old.

יא:ז וּמָתוֹק הָאוֹר וְטוֹב לַעֵינַיִם לִרְאוֹת אֶת־הַשָּׁמֶשׁ:

11:7 Sweet is the light, and how good for the eyes to see the sun.

Life is great. The *Targum* and Rashi take the first clause to refer to the light of Torah. But the *Targum* takes "the sun" in the last clause as a reference to the Divine Presence. Rashi, on the other hand, takes it to refer to a properly clarified statement of halachah. If this verse is linked to the next verse, then its literal meaning seems to hold sway over the commentators' interpretations.

יא:ח כִּי אִם־שָׁנִים הַרְבֵּה יִחְיֶה הָאָדָם בְּכֻלָּם יִשְׂמָח וְיִזְכֹּר אֶת־יְמֵי
הַחֹשֶׁךְ כִּי־הַרְבֵּה יִהְיוּ כָּל־שֶׁבָּא הָבֶל:

11:8 If you will live many years, then rejoice in them. Remember that the days of darkness will be many and everything that comes afterwards is meaningless.

Enjoy life while you can. Ibn Ezra presents a somewhat morose view of this verse. He claims that even though a person may "live many years" and might "rejoice in them," when that person contemplates "the days of darkness," that is, the grave, then even "the light" of the previous verse, which seemed "sweet," becomes bitter.

יא:ט שְׂמַח בָּחוּר בְּיַלְדוּתֶיךָ וִיטִיבְךָ לִבְּךָ בִּימֵי בְחוּרוֹתֶךָ וְהַלֵּךְ בְּדַרְכֵי לִבְּךָ וּבְמַרְאֵי עֵינֶיךָ וְדָע כִּי עַל־כָּל־אֵלֶּה יְבִיאֲךָ הָאֱלֹהִים בַּמִּשְׁפָּט:

11:9 BE HAPPY, YOUNG PERSON, WHILE YOU ARE YOUNG. ENJOY YOURSELF WHILE YOU'VE GOT YOUR YOUTH. GO WHEREVER YOUR HEART LEADS YOU AND YOUR EYES TAKE YOU—BUT KEEP IN MIND THAT FOR ALL THESE THINGS, GOD WILL CALL YOU TO JUDGMENT.

Rashi offers a charming perspective for the verse. It is like a parent telling a child, "You might as well sin because you will be punished for everything anyhow." Ibn Ezra notes that Kohelet begins this verse by telling his reader to enjoy the beginning of life, to rejoice in one's youth, even after he ends the previous verse with a description of life as *havel*, meaningless and useless.

יא:י וְהָסֵר כַּעַס מִלִּבֶּךָ וְהַעֲבֵר רָעָה מִבְּשָׂרֶךָ כִּי־הַיַּלְדוּת וְהַשַּׁחֲרוּת הָבֶל:

11:10 RID YOUR MIND OF ANXIETY. TAKE AWAY ANYTHING TROUBLING YOUR BODY, BECAUSE THE PRIME OF YOUTH EVAPORATES.

The two words *hayaldut v'hashacharut* (literally, "youth and dark hair") are taken by Koehler and Baumgartner (p. 1469) as a hendiadys to mean "the prime of youth." While we have elsewhere translated *havel*—the word that ends this verse—as "useless," here we have translated it as "evaporates" because its context suggests the transient nature of vapor. Rather than seeing this verse as an exhortation to enjoy oneself, Rashi takes it as a warning against doing so. He translates *kaas* (anxiety) as "anger, vexation" and *ruach* (wind, spirit) as "trouble," so that the verse communicates the message to avoid making God angry and to avoid the *yetzer hara* (the inclination to do evil).

The Numbers Seven and Eight

In his commentary on the Torah (p. 22), W. Gunther Plaut notes that the number seven is mentioned more than 500 times in the Bible. He presents two possible explanations for the importance of the number: the visibility of the sun, moon, and five planets and the fact that the lunar month falls into four quarters of seven days. Seven days make up a week, the Festival of Passover/Unleavened Bread lasts seven days (Exodus 13:6, 7; Leviticus 23:6), the Festival of Booths (Sukkot) lasts seven days (Leviticus 23:41), and one counts seven weeks from Passover to Shavuot, the Festival of Weeks (Leviticus 23:15). Seven years make up the Sabbatical year (Leviticus 25:4), and seven Sabbatical years make up the Jubilee year (Leviticus 25:8).

The observance of the Jubilee and the observance of the Festival of Weeks may be instructive in understanding the importance of the number eight. Jubilee is observed in the year following the completion of the counting of 7×7 years, that is, in the fiftieth year (Leviticus 25:9, 10), and Shavuot is observed on the day following the completion of the counting of 7×7 days, that is, on the fiftieth day (Leviticus 23:15, 16). It would seem that the unit, whether year or day, following the counting of seven units has some special, even mystical, importance. In this manner, we can understand the Eighth Day of Solemn Assembly (Leviticus 23:36), a festival whose meaning and origin is not otherwise given. It may be that the covenant of circumcision was set at eight days (Genesis 21:4) because it was seven days plus one day after birth (Leviticus 12:2, 3).

The Dry Bones Vision

Ezekiel was a prophet who lived in the sixth century B.C.E. His prophecies are contained in the biblical book that bears his name. When Nebuchadnezzar invaded Jerusalem, Ezekiel was deported to Babylonia along with King Jehoiachin of Judah and a large number of the inhabitants of Jerusalem. They were joined by later waves of exiles. As part of his message, Ezekiel tells the people that God intends to return Israel from its dominance by a foreign power, reunite the tribes, and bring them back to the Land of Israel. When the captives doubt Ezekiel's message and God's willingness to restore the people, the people's despair prompts the vision of a heap of dry bones that come back to life (Ezekiel 37:1–14). However unimaginable, this vision affirms the ingathering of the exiles.

Hendiadys

Hendiadys is a rhetorical form that expresses a single idea by two nouns instead of through the more common form of one noun and its qualifier. This method amplifies and adds force. A good example comes from Genesis 1:2: "The earth was without form and void *(tohu vavohu)*." To appreciate the use of the form in the Hebrew, the English might read, "The earth was a formless void."

GLEANINGS

Because I Know No Other Way

Here is the truth: I am discontent with the world the way it is. This is a funny thing to write—I feel so lucky to be alive, to feel the heat from the sun falling on my arm, to look at the flowers sent to me sitting on my desk. I have the ability to read, to write, to breathe . . . to be filled with awe and humility for feeling at one with the Universe in the here and now... and yet, I am discontent. I want there to be peace. I want God to be called in my image, in Hebrew and in English (and all languages). I want the birth of Jewish girls to be celebrated with equal communal joy as the birth of Jewish boys. I want all children to have food to eat tonight, and every night.

I am a changemaker because I want the world to be a better place for everyone. I am a changemaker because I have identified those issues about which I am most passionate, and I get pleasure from working on them and giving to them. I am a changemaker because I have found partners in my endeavors. And I am a changemaker because I recognize that I can use my brain, my time, and my money to indeed *make* the world a better place.

Sally Gottesman, "Changemaker Profile," fall 1998, www.mayan.org

Hard Work Is a Team Effort

Judaism describes a complex process of collective redemption; Jewish Messianism has numerous strands and is not easily described. But its basic structure goes something like this: first, the world was created whole; then it was broken; and in the future, it will be restored once more to wholeness. We can actually hear this process replicated in the notes of the *shofar*: *tefiah, shevarim, tekiah*—whole, broken, and whole. We live in the middle, in the fractured reality of human history, in the broken state of human imperfection. Our role as human beings is, with God's help, to fix the cracks within ourselves and within God's world.

The path to the Messianic future, the Jewish road to redemption, is paved with stories. They are not stories of superheroes or flawless characters. They are complex tales of human frailty, vulnerability, and deception, realistic stories of plain decency, simple acts of kindness and forgiveness. These stories teach us something about how we might redeem our broken selves and our broken world.

Marc J. Margolius, "Shaming the Sinner," in *Living Words: Best High Holiday Sermons of 5759,* ed. Susan Berrin (Newton, Mass.: JFL Books, 1999), 145–46

The Last Word

My mother, who turned eighty more than a few years ago, tells me that as you get older, it only gets worse: "No matter what you say, God always has the last word." That strikes me as wise, especially from a woman who has refined to high art the skill of getting in the last word. But it does make me wonder: What exactly is the "last word"?...

Before we begin our journey, we are one with all Creation. Once life begins, we find ourselves discrete, individuated, autonomous. And after the journey ends, God gets the last word: "Welcome." With some luck, we get glimmers of the great unity even during our lifetime. We realize that our life—and everything else—has all been part of the divine organism all along, that things are turning out "just the way God intends."

This is not to say that God is running the world like some overextended, occasionally under-performing puppeteer, depriving us of our freedom or moral responsibility. God is simply within all of it. And when we become aware of this, as we do during moments of great meaning or insight, it is as if God were the One who unites (and therefore runs) everything. Questions of free will and determinism become meaningless.

Everything exists within and derives its reality from God, including us. We are dimensions of the divine psyche, seeking to become fully self-aware. And, when we raise our consciousness, we not only realize that we have never really been apart from our divine Source at all, we realize that we also participate in the process itself. You may not be able to have an intimate relationship with such a God, but you are its pride and joy, its best hope.

My colleague, Rabbi Nehemiah Polen, taught me that the world simply is. It is the way it is supposed to be, the way it must be. Such a vision is achieved by a surrender of the ego, by submerging your self in the enveloping waters of divine being. We say the last word, "Oh my God!" to the universe and lose ourselves as we do so.

Lawrence Kushner, *Invisible Lines of Connection: Sacred Stories of the Ordinary* (Woodstock, Vt.: Jewish Lights Publishing, 1996), 144–45

CHAPTER TWELVE

יב:א וּזְכֹר אֶת־בּוֹרְאֶיךָ בִּימֵי בְּחוּרֹתֶיךָ עַד אֲשֶׁר לֹא־יָבֹאוּ יְמֵי הָרָעָה
וְהִגִּיעוּ שָׁנִים אֲשֶׁר תֹּאמַר אֵין־לִי בָהֶם חֵפֶץ:

12:1 Remember your Creator in the days of your youth, before the bad days arrive and the years come, when you are going to say, "I have no pleasure in them."

Many translate the word *bor'echa* as "your Creator" in an attempt to deepen the theological message of the book. Others suggest that it seems more consistent with the message of this chapter to read it as "your well-being" or even "your vigor." There are also those who suggest that it should be read as "your pit" as a reference to "the pit of death," a message that finds its origin in earlier chapters. Compare it to Proverbs 5:15, "Drink water out of your own cistern [pit] and running water out of your own well," where Rashi comments that it is a reference to the pleasure of sexuality. Here he argues that we should remember "your Creator" because at the end of life we approach the time of judgment. If this verse serves as an introduction to the rest of the chapter, it can simply be understood as an introduction to the physical metaphor that is continued throughout the chapter and therefore read, "before you lose your ability to taste." Rashi relates the verse to the statement in *Pirkei Avot* 3:1: "Akavya ben Mahalalel used to say, 'Reflect on three things and you will not come into the grasp of sin: know where you came from; know where you are going; and know in whose presence you will have to make an accounting." According to *Kohelet Rabbah* 12:2, Rabbi Joshua ben Levi of Sochnin said that Akavya deduced the three things from the word *bor'echa* (your Creator), which could also be read as *b'eirecha* (your well) or *borecha* (your pit). Thus, "where you came from" could be your well, that is, semen; "where you are going," your pit, that is, the grave; and "in whose presence you will have to make an accounting," your Creator.

יב:ב עַד אֲשֶׁר לֹא־תֶחְשַׁךְ הַשֶּׁמֶשׁ וְהָאוֹר וְהַיָּרֵחַ וְהַכּוֹכָבִים וְשָׁבוּ
הֶעָבִים אַחַר הַגָּשֶׁם:

12:2 Before the sun and the light, the moon and the stars grow dark, and the clouds come back after the rain.

The verse offers a description of the gloomy days that we have been told to expect. While we have translated these images independently in order to understand the

119

specific aspects of the metaphor, the verse could easily be translated as "the light of the moon and the stars" rather than treating sun and light separately. The image of rain and clouds is a thread throughout the text that helps identify the cultural context of the writer. If the metaphor understands a storm as the blotting out of a life, then the verse calls our attention to the darkening skies at the time of a storm. For the *Targum* and Rashi, who both take this verse as a metaphor, the "sun" refers to one's forehead, and the "light" refers to one's nose. The "moon" refers to the soul. The "stars" refer to the jaws, and the "clouds" refer to weeping, as a response to trouble. Although Ibn Ezra takes part of the verse literally, he offers a more eclectic view of the metaphor, understanding the verse in its entirety as a metaphor for death. He suggests that for the older person, here Kohelet disclosing his own struggle, the world grows dark, and even after a rain, it is not the sun but the clouds that appear. Ibn Ezra sees "the light" as that which appears just before sunrise. He thinks that as one dies, the world becomes progressively darker. It is as if initially the clouds had blocked the sun and the remaining light of day fades. Then one is left with the amount of light that the moon reflects. That too fades, and the moribund person is left with only the light of the stars. When even that fades—and it will—death ensues.

יב:ג בַּיּוֹם שֶׁיָּזֻעוּ שֹׁמְרֵי הַבַּיִת וְהִתְעַוְּתוּ אַנְשֵׁי הֶחָיִל וּבָטְלוּ הַטֹּחֲנוֹת
כִּי מִעֵטוּ וְחָשְׁכוּ הָרֹאוֹת בָּאֲרֻבּוֹת:

12:3 ON THE DAY WHEN THE GUARDIANS OF THE HOUSE SHAKE AND THE STRONG ARE STOOPED, AND THOSE WHO GRIND, GROWN FEW, STOP WORKING, AND THOSE WHO LOOK OUT THROUGH THE WINDOWS GROW DIM . . .

In order to picture the image that the author has presented, we have to imagine a multigenerational manor home of a wealthy family where there are virile, young guards who protect the inhabitants and a full staff of servants with particular responsibilities, and that there are individuals who peer through the window waiting for their spouses to come home. Literally, Kohelet imagined "the strong" as men, "those who grind" as women, and "those who look out" as ladies. The verse can be interpreted as a metaphor about the human body. The *Targum*, Rashi, and Ibn Ezra agree that this is a parable of the bodily ravages of old age, but differ in their interpretations of the details of the parable. For example, the *Targum* takes "the guardians of the house" as a reference to the legs. Rashi takes it to refer to the ribs, and Ibn Ezra thinks that it is related to the arms and the hands. For the *Targum*, the "strong" are the arms, but they are thighs for Rashi and Ibn Ezra. For all three commentators, "those who grind" are teeth. And "those who look out" are the eyes. Whichever specific parts of the body are meant, this perspective on the verse allows it to be read as Kohelet's commentary on the impact of old age on the body.

יב:ד וְסֻגְּרוּ דְלָתַיִם בַּשּׁוּק בִּשְׁפַל קוֹל הַטַּחֲנָה וְיָקוּם לְקוֹל הַצִּפּוֹר
וְיִשַּׁחוּ כָּל־בְּנוֹת הַשִּׁיר:

12:4 AND THE DOORS TO THE STREET ARE CLOSED AND
THE SOUND OF THE GRINDING MILL GROWS FAINT,
YET YOU GET STARTLED AT THE SOUND OF A BIRD AND
THE SOUND OF MUSICAL INSTRUMENTS BECOMES
INDISTINCT.

The metaphor continues, referring now to various orifices of the body. Although the *Targum*, Rashi, and Ibn Ezra agree that this verse is a metaphor that refers to the physical decline of the body over time, they disagree as to the precise elements to which the individual descriptions refer. Thus, the *Targum* takes "the doors" that "are closed" to mean that an old person has difficulty walking in the streets, while Rashi understands these doors to refer to constipation. Ibn Ezra understands "the doors" to mean the lips and "the grinding mill" to refer to digestion. The midrash on this verse from *Kohelet Rabbah* suggests that when older persons hear something as simple as a bird singing, they think that it is a robber. Some suggest that the strains of music (literally, "the daughters of music") refer to legs, but Rabbi Chiya (in *Kohelet Rabbah* 12:1) suggests that they are the kidneys, which offer up decisions to be made by the heart. Our translation of the last clause follows Rashi's interpretation: to an old person who is hard of hearing, even the sounds made by a musical instrument are not more recognizable than speech that is garbled.

יב:ה גַּם מִגָּבֹהַּ יִרָאוּ וְחַתְחַתִּים בַּדֶּרֶךְ וְיָנֵאץ הַשָּׁקֵד וְיִסְתַּבֵּל הֶחָגָב
וְתָפֵר הָאֲבִיּוֹנָה כִּי־הֹלֵךְ הָאָדָם אֶל־בֵּית עוֹלָמוֹ וְסָבְבוּ בַשּׁוּק
הַסֹּפְדִים:

12:5 YOU ARE AFRAID OF HEIGHTS, AND EVERY ROAD IS
FILLED WITH APPREHENSION; AND THE ALMOND TREE
BLOSSOMS, BUT THE GRASSHOPPER IS DRAGGED ALONG
AND THE CAPERBERRY DOESN'T WORK, FOR THE OLD
PERSON IS GOING TO HIS ETERNAL HOME AND THE
MOURNERS GO AROUND IN THE STREET.

While this verse presents a description of old age that is less than upbeat, the meanings of the idioms contained in the verse are no longer clear. The first part of the verse seems to indicate that the change of physical place is frightening for some older people. The midrash interprets this verse by suggesting that even if older people are invited to a banquet, they forgo it if they think that getting there might be dangerous. The second part of the verse contains three idioms. How one is interpreted will effect how the others are interpreted. If the middle part is a parable of the effect of aging on sexual ability and activity, if Rashi and Ibn Ezra are correct that the "grasshopper" refers to the penis, and if Rashi and Koehler and Baumgartner (p. 5) are correct that "the caperberry" was considered to be an aphrodisiac, then one may surmise that "the almond tree blossoms" refers to sexual desire, which, for the old man, may not be sufficient to effect an erection and cannot even be helped by an aphrodisiac. *Kohelet Rabbah* reads the almond trees midrashically as a reference to the "nut" of the spinal column, the only part—according to the rabbinic understanding of anatomy and physiology—that does not disintegrate after death. The grasshopper refers to the ankles, and the almond tree blossoms may refer to white hair. The verse ends with a suggestion that spring will surely come, but older adults will not experience it, because they will have gone to their eternal home.

יב:ו עַד אֲשֶׁר לֹא־יֵרָחֵק חֶבֶל הַכֶּסֶף וְתָרֻץ גֻּלַּת הַזָּהָב וְתִשָּׁבֶר כַּד עַל־הַמַּבּוּעַ וְנָרֹץ הַגַּלְגַּל אֶל־הַבּוֹר:

12:6 BEFORE THE SILVER CORD SNAPS AND THE GOLDEN BOWL CRASHES, THE PITCHER IS SHATTERED AT THE SPRING, AND THE WHEEL IS WRECKED AT THE WELL.

More imagery is offered for the end of life: a golden lamp held by a silver cord is shattered when the cord is severed, and the light goes out. Although Ibn Ezra takes the verse to be a metaphor of death and dying, he takes the plain sense of the verse to describe the process of drawing water from a well. A bucket connected to a rope passing over a pulley is sent into a well, the water of life and its symbol of redemption. If all things work correctly, one is able to draw water. However, if the rope breaks or if the wheel of the pulley fails, then the bucket crashes into the well and is broken. Thus, no water can be drawn. As Ibn Ezra understands the verse, with the onset of old age, all the parts of the human body break down: "the silver cord" is the spinal column, "the golden bowl" is the brain, "the pitcher" is the gallbladder, "the spring" is the liver, and "the wheel at the well" is the head. Rashi also takes the silver cord to be the spinal column, but he says that the golden bowl refers to the penis.

יב:ז וְיָשֹׁב הֶעָפָר עַל־הָאָרֶץ כְּשֶׁהָיָה וְהָרוּחַ תָּשׁוּב אֶל־הָאֱלֹהִים אֲשֶׁר נְתָנָהּ:

12:7 THE DUST RETURNS TO THE EARTH AS IT WAS, AND THE BREATH RETURNS TO GOD, WHO GAVE IT.

The first clause of the verse echoes Genesis 3:19; however, in the account of the creation of Adam in Genesis 2:7, it is *nishmat chayim* (the breath of life) that was blown into his nostrils rather than *ruach* (wind, breath), which is employed in this verse. However, the ancients understood breath the same way we do in the modern period: the ability to breathe is the mark of life. *Ruach* in the sense of breath is first found in the Noah story in Genesis 6:17 and 7:15. To some, this verse may seem to be at odds with the earlier statements made by Kohelet in 3:19–21. It would seem that Kohelet changed his perspective once again. However, the next verse brings us back to his earlier perspective.

$$\text{יב:ח הֲבֵל הֲבָלִים אָמַר הַקּוֹהֶלֶת הַכֹּל הָבֶל:}$$

12:8 "TOTAL USELESSNESS," SAYS KOHELET, "EVERYTHING IS USELESS."

If death brings a final judgment, then perhaps everything is useless. Some scholars argue that because of the final despair or cynicism that is offered in this verse, a pious editor must have added the epilogue that follows to make Kohelet's sentiments more acceptable. Others suggest that Kohelet, though referring to himself in the third person as might naturally befit his self-described royal status, came to the final conclusion on his own at the end of his life. A third possibility is that the epilogue was written by a student or disciple who knew Kohelet well and drew the conclusions on behalf of his teacher.

$$\text{יב:ט וְיֹתֵר שֶׁהָיָה קֹהֶלֶת חָכָם עוֹד לִמַּד־דַּעַת אֶת־הָעָם וְאִזֵּן וְחִקֵּר}$$
$$\text{תִּקֵּן מְשָׁלִים הַרְבֵּה:}$$

12:9 KOHELET NOT ONLY WAS A WISE PERSON, HE ALSO TAUGHT THE PEOPLE KNOWLEDGE, AND AFTER PROBING THINGS FAIRLY, HE COMPOSED MANY PARABLES.

The verse begins, *V'yoteir,* "In addition to this, let me say further...." As noted above, scholars argue that Kohelet does not appear to be the author of this verse. Perhaps the message of the editor here is: Kohelet was wise, so don't write off what he said. He had made a career of teaching and instruction and therefore speaks with authority. The verb *izein* (to act fairly, equitably, in a balanced manner) comes from the noun *moznaim* (scales). It is also related to the noun *oznayim* (ears, handles). Rashi quotes the midrash (*Shir HaShirim Rabbah* 1:5) that Solomon (whom he and the tradition thought to be the author of Kohelet) made "handles" for the Torah so that it might be better grasped. Ibn Ezra derives *izein* both from *ozen* (ear) and from *moznaim.* From the first, he understands the verb to mean either "compose songs or poems" or "to sing" or "to declaim them." From the second, he understands the verb to mean "to compose the balances of wisdom."

יב:י בִּקֵּשׁ קֹהֶלֶת לִמְצֹא דִּבְרֵי־חֵפֶץ וְכָתוּב יֹשֶׁר דִּבְרֵי אֱמֶת:

12:10 KOHELET TRIED TO FIND WORDS THAT WERE USEFUL
AND RECORDED CORRECTLY WORDS OF TRUTH.

This obviously continues the opinion of the editor. The difference between the world of Rashi and the world of Ibn Ezra can be seen in their differing interpretations of *divrei cheifetz* (words that were useful). According to Rashi, such words refer to the *halachah l'Moshe miSinai* (the halachah given to Moses at Sinai), that is, an ancient but binding tradition that lacks a scriptural base. According to Ibn Ezra, the words refer to Supreme Wisdom, why things are the way they are, that is, philosophy. It is no surprise that Rashi notes that "words of truth" that were "recorded correctly" refers to the Written Torah and the Prophets. Whatever the specific reference, the author reminds us that these wise sayings should not be taken lightly.

יב:יא דִּבְרֵי חֲכָמִים כַּדָּרְבֹנוֹת וּכְמַשְׂמְרוֹת נְטוּעִים בַּעֲלֵי אֲסֻפּוֹת נִתְּנוּ
מֵרֹעֶה אֶחָד:

12:11 THE WORDS OF THE WISE ARE LIKE GOADS, AND LIKE
FIXED NAILS ARE THE COLLECTED SAYINGS. THEY COME
FROM ONE SHEPHERD.

This verse is made difficult by the words *baalei asupot*, a phrase not found elsewhere in the Bible. The *Targum* translates the term by *v'rabanai Sanhedrin marei hilch'tin umedrashin* (the scholars of the Sanhedrin, masters of law and lore). Thus, the *Targum* takes the phrase as "masters of assemblies." Rashi understands the word to refer to "nails with heads." Ibn Ezra, focusing on *asupot* (that which is gathered in), takes the words to refer to books that are composed of selections of other books. We have followed Koehler and Baumgartner (p. 75), which emends *baalei* to *mishlei* and understands the two words to mean "collection of sayings." A clever saying was held to be something sharp. According to Ibn Ezra, the reason that God is here called Shepherd is that both cattle and humans require goads: the cattle to move on a road, humans to move toward the truth.

יב:יב וְיֹתֵר מֵהֵמָּה בְּנִי הִזָּהֵר עֲשׂוֹת סְפָרִים הַרְבֵּה אֵין קֵץ וְלַהַג הַרְבֵּה
יְגִעַת בָּשָׂר:

12:12 MORE THAN ANYTHING ELSE, MY YOUNG FRIEND,
WATCH OUT. THERE IS NO LIMIT TO THE MAKING OF
BOOKS, AND TOO MUCH STUDY WEARS OUT THE FLESH.

Ibn Ezra understands *asot s'farim* (making of books) as *maasot s'farim* (from making books), a warning against making books. They don't last, and neither does the wisdom they contain. He also notes that *lahag* occurs only here and its meaning of "study" is deduced from its Arabic cognate. Based on this verse, it appears that the writer of the epilogue was in a far different conceptual world than was the writer of the book. Kohelet would hardly have opposed the making of books or study.

יב:יג סוֹף דָּבָר הַכֹּל נִשְׁמָע אֶת־הָאֱלֹהִים יְרָא וְאֶת־מִצְוֺתָיו שְׁמוֹר
כִּי־זֶה כָּל־הָאָדָם:

12:13 THE LAST WORD, EVERYTHING HAVING BEEN SAID AND DONE: REVERE GOD AND KEEP THE COMMANDMENTS, FOR THIS APPLIES TO EVERY PERSON.

According to Rashi, the last clause means that each person was created to observe the divine commandments. On the surface, it seems that the writer of the epilogue was troubled by the general approach of the Book of *Kohelet*. This might indeed be the case, since the epilogue writer's approach concentrates on a return to faith and observance. However, the oscillation between faith and skepticism is a familiar posture throughout Jewish literature. The recognition of this duality is one of the significant gifts offered by *Kohelet*.

יב:יד כִּי אֶת־כָּל־מַעֲשֶׂה הָאֱלֹהִים יָבִא בְמִשְׁפָּט עַל כָּל־נֶעְלָם אִם־טוֹב
וְאִם־רָע:
סוֹף דָּבָר הַכֹּל נִשְׁמָע אֶת־הָאֱלֹהִים יְרָא וְאֶת־מִצְוֺתָיו שְׁמוֹר
כִּי־זֶה כָּל־הָאָדָם:

12:14 GOD WILL BRING TO JUDGMENT EVERY ACT, WHETHER GOOD OR BAD, EVEN THAT WHICH IS HIDDEN.

Rashi understands "that which is hidden" as that which is inadvertent. Ibn Ezra concludes his commentary on *Kohelet* with the following benediction: "Praised is the One who knows the truth and for whose mercies would I implore that my errors might be atoned for. May God so awake my glory that God may make me know the path of life." When this text is read publicly in the synagogue for Sukkot, verse 13 is repeated after verse 14, so that the public reading ends on a positive, conciliatory note, rather than one that evokes harsh punishment. This is called a *n'chemta*, a consolation, which we have translated: "The last word, everything having been said and done: Revere God and keep the commandments, for this applies to every person."

Old Age

It takes more than just the accumulation of years to grow old. Old age is an art that takes years to perfect. We don't just wake up old one morning. We *grow* older by taking the experiences of living and slowly weaving them over time into a tapestry of life. Even with all those years of journey under our feet, we never really get it just right. So we keep working at it. That's the miracle of life. The Rabbis of *Pirkei Avot* understood it best when they considered the question "Who is wise?" Their response: "Those who learn from everyone" (*Pirkei Avot* 4:1). The opportunity old age gives us is unavailable at any other time of our lives. We take what we have learned and through the prism of our weathered souls gain a unique perspective on living, one that we can share with others, especially those who come after us. When we can live the wisdom we have learned, we can indeed consider ourselves old. And that's the true blessing.

Nechemta

Nechemta literally means "consolation." The Rabbis employed the notion that the public reading from the Prophets should not end on a note of rebuke, but on a note of hope. This came to be known as *nechemta*, "consolation." As a result, verses often are repeated, even if they appear out of order. The term became applied more generally in Jewish culture to refer to any act or message of consolation.

Life Review

Social gerontologists speak of life review as an opportunity to look back on our lives, to assess and access its essential meaning. It is one of those human activities of self-reflection that separates us from all of God's other creations. In other words, it is what makes us human: that ability to go outside of ourselves in order to penetrate more deeply inside. Through the process, we are provided with focus for our lives. We gain insight and direction in our lives. Life review is not restricted to any one particular age or station in life. We usually engage in life review at special times, in anticipation of or after significant changes like milestone birthdays. Other occasions might include job changes, retirement, or a move to a new place. Sometimes this process of introspection takes the form of a mini–life review, flashes of insight when we would least expect them. One of the Chasidic rebbes used to teach that there are some moments in our lives when the total purpose of our existence is revealed to us. However, life review is most associated with the process of growing older (note the word "growing"), because that's when there is so much substance to evaluate and consider. Through a life review, we come to understand the very purpose for which God placed us on this earth in the first place. Then we face the ultimate challenge: now that we know, what do we do about it?

GLEANINGS

A Happy Death

Rabbi Yitz Greenberg teaches that "the shock of death reminds us that time is too short to waste and too short to let pride and despair trap one in a life pattern with little in it to savor and respect." The awareness of death puts life into bold capital letters. Suddenly "no aspect of life can be taken for granted, (and) no feature of our (personality) is either eternal or absolutely necessary" (*The Jewish Way* by Irving Greenberg, pp. 200–203). But we're fighting an uphill battle, because the power of bad patterns is that they convince us that change is impossible; that our relationship with our sibling, spouse, friend, co-worker, is just...the way it is. And now Yom Kippur appears as a challenge to our lazy and cowardly excuses. Today forces us to address our own mortality. It serves as a reminder that we don't have forever and that *teshuvah is* possible. Socrates once said, "The unexamined life is not worth living." Rabbi Greenberg reinterprets this Jewishly by saying, "To live the unexamined life is not really living," warning that, "if (we) are the same as (we) were last year, (we) have died a little in the interim" (ibid, reworded). In other words, a life without *teshuvah* leads to death, and Yom Kippur, the day of *teshuvah*, is our wake-up call to life.

Michelle Missaghieh, "Yom Kippur and Death: Have a Happy Death" in *Living Words:*
Best High Holiday Sermons of 5759, ed. Susan Berrin (Newton, Mass.: JFL Books, 1999), 160–61

Our Contribution

In the prime of life, we seek a place to leave our mark. We want the world to be different as a result of our having lived. We could leave a physical mark by, say, contributing a pebble to the cairn built by nomads and shepherds, to show that we've passed through. But even elaborate buildings crumble. Most of us have lived or will live to see something achieved undone. If work were only about tasks accomplished, then the undoing of our life's work (or even of a lesser accomplishment) would lead us to a sense of futility. But if our understanding of work expands to include a place where we can grow, be transformed, and even encounter the Holy, then we can accept that at least some of our undertakings can never be undone.

The most satisfying realm in which we can make our mark is in the lives of the people we have touched in some significant way through the work of loving, nurturing, and teaching. Somehow, the energy and life we invest in working with others can start a transformative process and help create worlds of meaning and connectedness.

Carol Ochs, *Our Lives as Torah: Finding God in Our Own Stories*
(San Francisco: Jossey-Bass, 2001), 104–5

Old Age as Sabbath

In the Messianic thought of Judaism (not in the contemporary Jewish community, regrettably), the individual who attains old age is not only not degraded but is honored. The aged can now address themselves to high purposes such as the study of God's word and the purification and refinement of the soul of man. Nothing is lost if man does not have to work; he may still enjoy the Sabbath. As a matter of fact, for him each day is now a Sabbath. The passage in Genesis (3:17) presenting man as toiling life-long to earn his bread has not been taken in Judaism as establishing work as anything like an absolute value. Labor does not serve the function of compensating or atoning for guilt. Necessary as work may be, it is not, as Rabbi [Norman] Lamm wrote, "an autonomous virtue" ["Ethics and Leisure," in *Faith and Doubt* (New York: Ktav, 1986), 187–209]. It may be true that it is "natural" for man to work—in Genesis 2:15 he is enjoined to till and keep the Garden of Eden—but it is not the necessary condition for salvation.

As the Sabbath is the climax of creation, so the time of maturity represents the highest point of man's development. In the "Sabbath days" of his old age, man has the opportunity not to rest, although he may do that, but to "refresh himself." In the passage in Exodus 31:17 God rests and is refreshed. What God does is paradigmatic for man. Resting, in that passage, signifies cessation from work; being refreshed refers to activity that is creative and active and yields a sense of renewal and inspiration. Ceasing to work does not mean becoming idle or aimless. With leisure comes the opportunity for another kind of activity, the goal of which is the cultivation of one's soul and its potentialities.

Robert L. Katz, "Jewish Values and Sociopsychological Perspectives on Aging,"
in *Toward a Theology of Aging,* ed. Seward Hiltner (New York: Human Sciences Press, 1975), 148–49

Reconciliation

Reconciliation with human limitations brought Qoheleth to the utmost spiritual experience. Here, an individual's relationship with the divine received a sense of awe and humility. The adoration of God and the following in his ways were the spiritual means which Qoholeth correlated with the pursuit of happiness. Thus, he taught that, in youth, the recognition that old age was imminent and life was finite should become the impetus to motivate one's quest for happiness. For true joy was the means by which humanity could recognize the greatness of God: the more one enjoyed the goodness of life the more one appreciated the goodness of God. It is through Qoheleth's teaching that awareness of the limiting characteristics of life brings one to more fully appreciate the beauty in life, the joy in living in the present, and thereby the closeness one can feel with the Creator himself.

Rachel Zohar Dulin, *A Crown of Glory: A Biblical View of Aging*
(New York: Paulist Press, 1988), 46–47

Bibliography

Eichhorn, David Max. *Musings of the Old Professor: The Meaning of Koheles, a New Translation of and Commentary on the Book of Ecclesiastes.* New York: Jonathan David, 1963.

Fox, Michael. ''Frame Narrative and Composition in the Book of Qohelet.'' *Hebrew Union College Annual* 48 (1977): 83–106.

Gordis, Robert. *Koheleth, the Man and His World: A Study of Ecclesiastes.* 3d ed. New York: Schocken Books, 1968.

_____. *The Wisdom of Ecclesiastes.* New York: Behrman House, 1945.

Koehler, L., and W. Baumgartner. *The Hebrew and Aramaic Lexicon of the Old Testament.* 5 Vols. Trans. and ed. M. E. J. Richardson et al. Leiden; New York: E. J. Brill, 1994–2000.

Levy, Benjamin. *A Faithful Heart: Preparing for the High Holy Days.* New York: UAHC Press, 2001.

Shapiro, Rami. *The Way of Solomon: Finding Joy and Contentment in the Wisdom of Ecclesiastes.* San Francisco: HarperSanFrancisco, 2000.

Biographies

Rabbi Bradley Shavit Artson is dean of the Ziegler Rabbinical School at the University of Judaism in Los Angeles.

Susan Berrin is the editor of *Sh'ma: A Journal of Jewish Responsibility.*

Rabbi Terry Bookman is senior rabbi, Temple Beth Am, Miami, Florida.

Dr. Eugene B. Borowitz is the Sigmund L. Falk Distinguished Professor of Education and Jewish Religious Thought at Hebrew Union College–Jewish Institute of Religion, where he has taught since 1962. He is the author of numerous books, including *Renewing the Covenant,* and the first person to receive a National Foundation for Jewish Culture Achievement Award in Scholarship for work in the field of Jewish thought.

Rabbi Lester Bronstein is lecturer in rabbinics at Hebrew Union College–Jewish Institute of Religion, New York, and rabbi of Bet Am Shalom Synagogue in White Plains, New York.

Rabbi Norman J. Cohen is professor of midrash and provost of Hebrew Union College–Jewish Institute of Religion.

Anita Diamant is the author of the best-selling *The Red Tent.*

Rabbi Wayne Dosick is one of the leading teachers of Jewish spirituality in North America. He is the spiritual leader of the Elijah Minyan in San Diego, a lecturer at the University of San Diego, and the author of numerous works that reclaim the spiritual dimension of Jewish religious practice and belief.

Dr. Rachel Zohar Dulin is professor of Hebrew and Bible at Spertus Institute of Judaica in Chicago, Illinois.

Rabbi David Ellenson is president of Hebrew Union College–Jewish Institute of Religion and I. H. and Anna Grancell Professor of Jewish Religious Thought at its Los Angeles campus.

Rabbi Edward Feinstein is rabbi at Valley Beth Shalom in Encino, California.

Rabbi Elyse D. Frishman is rabbi of Congregation B'nai Jeshurun: The Barnert Memorial Temple in Franklin Lakes, New Jersey.

Rabbi Elyse Goldstein is director of KOLEL: The Adult Center for Liberal Jewish Learning near Toronto, Ontario.

Sally Gottesman is a consultant to not-for-profit organizations. She serves on the boards of the Jewish Women's Archives, the Jewish Funders Network, and the Reconstructionist Rabbinical College, where she chairs Kolot: The Center for Jewish Women's and Gender Studies.

Rabbi Ben Kamin is rabbi of Temple Beth Israel in San Diego, California.

Rabbi Robert L. Katz was professor of human relations at Hebrew Union College–Jewish Institute of Religion, Cincinnati.

Rabbi Peter S. Knobel is the senior rabbi of Beth Emet: The Free Synagogue in Evanston, Illinois.

Rabbi Lawrence Kushner is the rabbi-in-residence at Hebrew Union College–Jewish Institute of Religion. He was the spiritual leader of Congregation Beth El of Sudbury, Massachusetts for twenty-five years and is the author of numerous books and articles, including *God Was in This Place and I, i Did Not Know.*

Rabbi Benjamin Levy is the rabbi of the Monroe Township Jewish Center in New Jersey. He is the author of *A Faithful Heart: Preparing for the High Holy Days.*

Rabbi Jane Rachel Littman is the rabbi-educator of Congregation Beth El in Berkeley, California.

Rabbi Marc J. Margolius is the religious leader of Congregation Beth Am Israel in Philadelphia.

Rabbi Michelle Missaghieh is the associate rabbi of Temple Israel in Hollywood in Los Angeles.

Rabbi Leon A. Morris is the director of the Skirball Center for Adult Jewish Learning at Temple Emanu-El in New York City, New York.

Dr. Carol Ochs is director of graduate studies and adjunct associate professor of Jewish religious thought at Hebrew Union College–Jewish Institute of Religion, New York.

Rabbi Kerry M. Olitzky is the executive director of the Jewish Outreach Institute. Previously, he was the vice president of the Wexner Heritage Foundation.

Judy Petsonk has been involved in the Havurah and Jewish feminist movements for twenty years. She is a former teacher and newspaper reporter. Currently, she lectures and conducts workshops on spirituality and intermarriage, as well as other topics, in synagogues and other institutions throughout the United States.

Rabbi Bernard S. Raskas is rabbi laureate at Temple Aaron in St. Paul, Minnesota.

Dr. Ellis Rivkin is Adolph S. Ochs Professor Emeritus at Hebrew Union College–Jewish Institute of Religion, Cincinnati.

Rabbi Jeffrey Salkin is the senior rabbi of the Community Synagogue in Port Washington, New York.

Rabbi Harold M. Schulweis is rabbi at Valley Beth Shalom in Encino, California. He is the author of *Finding Each Other in Judaism: Meditations on the Life Cycle from Birth to Immortality* (New York: UAHC Press, 2001).

Lynn Schusterman is co-founder and president of the Charles and Lynn Schusterman Family Foundation of Tulsa, Oklahoma.

Frances Weinman Schwartz is a teacher of adult Jewish education and Holocaust studies and the producer of a monthly book discussion program sponsored by New York Kollel.

Dr. Byron L. Sherwin is an educator and theologian who specializes in ethics and Kabbalah. He is the author of numerous books and articles including *Crafting the Soul: Creating Your Life as a Work of Art* and *No Religion Is an Island*. Dr. Sherwin is vice president of the Spertus Institute of Jewish Studies in Chicago.

Howard M. Steiermann is a real estate consultant and a lay leader at Congregation Sha'ar Zahav in San Francisco, California.

Rabbi Ira F. Stone is spiritual leader of Temple Beth Zion–Beth Israel in Philadelphia.

Rabbi Allan C. Tuffs is rabbi of Temple Beth El in Hollywood, Florida.

Rabbi Eric H. Yoffie is president of the Union of American Hebrew Congregations.